A Gospel Christmas

Our Journey Connecting Santa and His Elf to the Story of our Savior

JENNIFER MOYE

ISBN 978-1-68197-273-2 (paperback)
ISBN 978-1-68197-274-9 (digital)

All scripture quotations, unless otherwise indicated, are taken from the Holy Bible, NEW INTERNATIONAL READER'S VERSION®. Copyright © 1996, 1998 Biblica. All rights reserved throughout the world. Used by permission of Biblica.

All images taken by Micheal Lynn Photography and property of Jennifer Moye.

Christian Faith Publishing, Inc.
296 Chestnut Street
Meadville, PA 16335
www.christianfaithpublishing.com

Printed in the United States of America

Dedicated to Johnathan, Ian, and Jacob.
For constantly teaching me what it means to love
and be loved by the King of Heaven.
I love you more than you can imagine.

Special thanks to Amanda and Shannon
For gently "nudging" me to step into my next highest place
with Christ, and for your countless words of encouragement. You make me a better daughter of the King.

To order the craft kits used in this book I encourage you to visit:
www.25daysofchrist.com

am so excited to share with you this wonderful journey through the life of Jesus! When we began this devotional series, I had no idea what a great impact it would have not only on our boys, but on myself and others as well. Since having kids, it has been increasingly difficult to rein in the "holiday" chaos. Presents, lights, parties, decorations, hosting family, and all the "plastic stuff" we need to spend an entire paycheck on can get out of control in the blink of an eye. How do I teach my children the true meaning of Christmas in a world that calls it a "holiday"? How do I keep all the fun and point them to our Savior at the same time? If you have struggled with these questions then you are in the right place! Hang with me over the next twenty-five days and we will celebrate together as we watch our children realize the true meaning of Christmas.

In years past, we have used the famous Elf on the Shelf routine with the boys, and to be quite honest I found myself feeling . . . guilty—guilty about tricking them into a pressure situation where someone was constantly watching them and if they dare to act like actual children, they would be at risk of being on the naughty list. It just didn't sit right for me. We want our boys to experience the fun and excitement of Santa and all that goes along with that, but we also want them to grow up knowing that the birth of our Savior is the first and foremost reason for the Christmas season. I believe we have found a great way to integrate the Elf and Santa into our learning about Jesus's birth. Over the next few weeks I hope to share with you our journey!

Elfie made his first appearance on the last day of November. He brought with him a letter from Santa and a box of Elfie treat bags. The letter says that Santa is no longer keeping a naughty and nice list because he has come to realize that we are all naughty at times no matter how hard we try. Elfie is a little naughty so he is being sent to us by Santa so that we can help teach Elfie about grace and about the love that Jesus gives us even when we don't deserve it. So no more naughty or nice list; in its place is grace. Praise God for His never-ending unconditional grace!

With the bags that Elfie brought us we made a yummy batch of reindeer chow to be able to give away to friends and others that we encounter this month. We brought out a box of Christmas cards and decided each day we would try to give a card and a bag of treats to someone, and we would also make it a point to serve someone each day this month.

I need to be very honest with you right now. I am no super mom. I forgot to move Elfie on more than one occasion. I got about half of my ideas for his actions from random Pinterest pages that some other brilliant super mom came up with. If you are going to do the next twenty-five days with Elfie in tow, please do not get caught up in the details of where Elfie moves to and what he is doing. I am begging you, the objective here is not how original or involved you can make your elf be. Keep focused on the Scripture lessons as they are the most central part of this journey. When you forget to move the elf, or you wake up at two AM and remember, don't freak out. Remember, he is not reporting back to Santa every night since there is no naughty list. If he is in the same place, just go with it. I did it, you will do it, and it's okay.

I set out on this journey to help my kids be more focused on Christ this Christmas season. By December 25, I realized how much I needed to hear the words I read and spoke to them. I watched my boys not only serve others in a way I'd never seen before, but I also watched their eyes being opened to the gospel of Jesus Christ in a way they never had. I was moved time and time again at my boys teaching me what I had intended to teach them. I can't wait to share this journey with you and I pray your family sees and hears our Heavenly Father move in ways that only He can! Thank you for joining us and Merry Christmas!

Day 1

IT STARTED WITH A BABY

This morning we woke to find Elfie on the dining room table riding in style on the back of Sven from the movie *Frozen*. He also left a small pile of "chocolate chips" trailing behind him. That naughty Elf! He had taken out our large family Bible and had a little red sack with him that contained a passage of Scripture and everything we needed to make our first ornament for our small Christmas tree which we decided to put up on the kitchen island.

> *In those days Caesar Augustus issued a decree that a census should be taken of the entire Roman world. (This was the first census that took place while Quirinius was governor of Syria.) And everyone went to their own town to register. So Joseph also went up from the town of Nazareth in Galilee to Judea, to Bethlehem the town of David, because he belonged to the house and line of David. He went there to register with Mary, who was pledged to be married to him and was expecting a child. While they were there, the time came for the baby to be*

*born, and she gave birth to her firstborn, a son. She
wrapped him in cloths and placed him in a manger,
because there was no guest room available for them.
(Luke 2:1–7)*

Our ornament for today was a star. As we were painting the star
a bright yellow and fixing the twine around the top, we talked about
what it must have been like to travel so far without having a hotel
room to stay in. We talked about what it would be like to have to
stop in the middle of our road trip and sleep in a barn with all the
animals. How scary it must have been for Mary and Joseph to have
their first baby there with no family or friends or doctors around. I
told the boys stories about when I was pregnant with them and how
I worried and ran to the doctor over every little thing. I told them
how nervous and scared I was to go through labor and delivery. I
can't imagine the anxiety Mary must have had. It is truly amazing to
see the faces of our boys turn to genuine concern when they start to
think about how things might have been.

The boys were super excited to hang their ornament on the tree
and could not wait to brag about it to Daddy! The next item on their
agenda was to decide what to do with our gift bags of goodies we had
made yesterday. Though it was cold and rainy outside, Johnathan
was convinced we needed to go outside and start handing it out to
the neighbors. I love his big heart. The first thing we did was put a
card and bag in our mailbox for our mail carrier. The boys were so
concerned about it being out there all day I believe they must have
run out to check on it at least a half-dozen times. Finally they came
screaming in the house, "He took it! He took it!"

Later this evening we decided to go out for dinner and thought
we would take our goodies to share with our server at the restaurant.
Johnathan had the honor of handing the card and bag over to our
sweet waitress. She was so surprised that someone would bring her
something special. The boys' faces lit up with pride that they had
made someone happy with something they made.

As we start this twenty-five-day journey together, I challenge
you each day to find a way to bring a gift of service to someone. The

baby Jesus born in a manger was the greatest gift humanity could ever dream of. The sacrifice that Mary gave by being obedient and trusting in what God had revealed to her is astounding to me. Would I be that faithful if I were in her shoes? What an example she is of a loving and sacrificial mommy for us. Through all of her human concerns and worries, she was calm and peaceful. She made the best of her circumstances and honored God through her obedience and care for sweet baby Jesus.

Day 2

CELEBRATION IN THE FIELD

This morning we found Elfie surrounded by a herd of sheep! And by sheep I really mean a bunch of cotton balls with black Sharpie dots on them that kind of look like eyes. He also had a shepherd's rod in his hand. And by shepherd's rod I really mean a wooden skewer I found in the back of the silverware drawer. In his bag we found our craft materials and our Scripture for the day.

> *And there were shepherds living out in the fields nearby, keeping watch over their flocks at night. An angel of the Lord appeared to them, and the glory of the Lord shone around them, and they were terrified. But the angel said to them, "Do not be afraid. I bring you good news that will cause great joy for all the people. Today in the town of David a Savior has been born to you; he is the Messiah, the Lord. This will be a sign to you: You will find a baby wrapped in cloths and lying in a manger." Suddenly a great company of the heavenly host appeared with the angel, praising God and saying, "Glory to God*

*in the highest heaven, and on earth peace to those on
whom his favor rests." (Luke 2:8–14)*

What an amazing scene this must have been! We had such a
great time acting out this scene a little bit. We went down to our
basement, which is also our homeschool room, and turned off all the
lights. The boys got in their secret hiding place under the stairs and
piled all their pillows up around them as if they were a herd of sheep
surrounding them. We imagined we were in a field at night watching
over our sheep, minding our own business. Then all of a sudden I
turned the bright lights on and said in an alarmingly loud, overacting
voice, "Behold! Do not be afraid! I bring you good news." The boys
jumped at the suddenness of the light and sound. It was such a great
moment of putting ourselves in the "shoes" of the shepherds. What
must they have thought? Were they afraid? Excited?

We then proceeded to march around the house screaming,
"Glory to God in the highest! Peace on Earth! Jesus is born!" I have
no idea why we were screaming and marching. I just went with it.

Our ornament for the day was to paint and assemble a shepherd. This one was a bit more involved than the star from yesterday
as it involved more paint, a hot glue gun, and a small amount of
artisticness, which I do not possess. Thankfully our boys are not old
enough to realize all of my shortcomings and were once again very
proud of their little token for the day. We painted the face and body
of our little shepherd and then took a small piece of cloth and glued
it on top of his head to make a cover.

After all of the fun excitement from the morning, we had to
take Ian up to Cincinnati Children's for his usual eye appointment.
We decided to take a few cards and goodie bags with us to see who
we could find to bless. As you might expect, there was not a shortage
of people who needed a pick-me-up in that place. We handed out
goodie bags and Christmas cards to several nurses and of course our
doctor. Everyone was so surprised and happy to receive such a gift.
My very favorite memory from today was at the lab. Ian has to have
labs done every month to check his liver function because of the
medicine he is on for his Juvenile Arthritis. Since he does this every

month he totally knows what is coming when we head that direction. It is always heartbreaking to see him dread the poke. This sweet nurse today took her time with him and tried to calm him. After everything was over and the tears were dried, Ian reached inside my bag and pulled out the last treat bag and card and gave it to the nurse who had just, in his mind, inflicted pain on him. She got tears in her eyes and was so moved. I have to admit, I started tearing up as well. She told him how blessed this act made her feel and how much she appreciated that he would choose her to give his gift to.

I couldn't help but watch Ian's act of kindness and forgiveness and think of our wonderful Savior. From Ian's four-year-old world, this person had just caused him tears and pain, yet he still chose to bless her and love her anyway. Isn't this just like God's love and amazing grace for us? We are so undeserving of the grace He pours over us yet He chooses to bless us anyway! There is no greater joy as a mommy than seeing Jesus through my boys! Ian is such a trooper. Through all of his health struggles and pain, he is so strong and has such a huge heart for others who are hurting. It makes me want to march through the halls shouting, "Glory to God in the highest!"

What will you shout "Glory to God in the highest" about today? No matter what you are facing, God is here and He is right here with you! Give Him glory today despite your circumstances, for He is worthy.

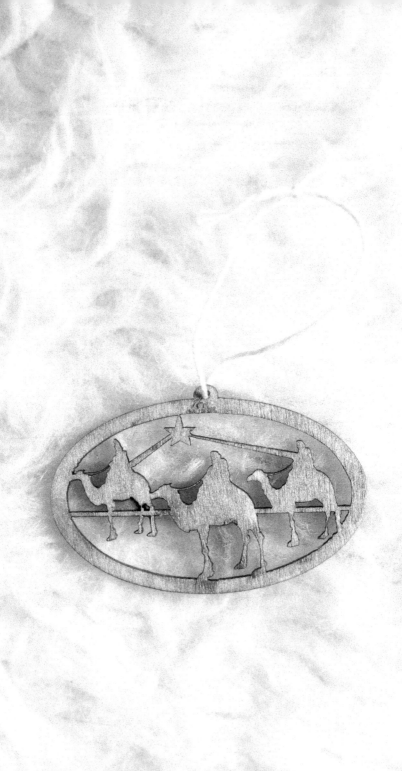

Day 3

THERE'S A BAD GUY!

So I need to be honest with you. Today was a wild and stressful day. Today I was not super mom. Today I kept my kids alive, and I feel okay with that. If you are like me it is all too often that you read some mommy blog and think, "She is super mom." I am not that kind of blogger or mom! Today was rough. Today I needed God's grace. Nothing super bad happened; it was just a chaotic day with fussy boys and a tired, impatient mommy. There seemed to be a million things pulling at us and distracting us from our Christmas message. That's how the enemy works, you know? He is pretty good at sending us lots of "good" pressures and tasks in order to distract us from the "great" things God has in store for us to learn and experience.

Will you stand with me today and refuse to let the enemy win?

Today we found Elfie in a big messy pile of wrapping paper, presents, and tied up in some ribbon. He is such a mess maker! In his little bag he had materials to make a new ornament and the Scripture.

> *Jesus was born in Bethlehem in Judea. This happened while Herod was king of Judea. After Jesus' birth, Wise Men from the east came to Jerusalem.*

They asked, "Where is the child who has been born to be king of the Jews? We saw his star when it rose. Now we have come to worship him."

When King Herod heard about it, he was very upset. Everyone in Jerusalem was troubled too. So Herod called together all the chief priests of the people. He also called the teachers of the law. He asked them where the Messiah was going to be born. "In Bethlehem in Judea," they replied. "This is what the prophet has written. He said, 'But you, Bethlehem, in the land of Judah, are certainly not the least important among the towns of Judah. A ruler will come out of you. He will rule my people Israel like a shepherd [Micah 5:2].'"

Then Herod secretly called for the Wise Men. He found out from them exactly when the star had appeared. He sent them to Bethlehem. He said, "Go and search carefully for the child. As soon as you find him, report it to me. Then I can go and worship him too."

After the Wise Men had listened to the king, they went on their way. The star they had seen when it rose went ahead of them. It finally stopped over the place where the child was. When they saw the star, they were filled with joy. The Wise Men went to the house. There they saw the child with his mother Mary. They bowed down and worshiped him. Then they opened their treasures. They gave him gold, frankincense and myrrh. But God warned them in a dream not to go back to Herod. So they returned to their country on a different road. (Matthew 2:1–12)

Our ornament was a cutout of the three wise men riding on their camels with the star high in the sky. We decided to paint in shiny gold to signify the fancy gifts they brought to baby Jesus. I was surprised how quickly the boys identified the "bad guy" in this story. Children have a way of knowing those things, don't they? We talked a lot about how the star and the shepherd we had made in days 1 and 2 tied into this story. They were amazed to discover how connected the stories in the Bible were and how they are really all part of one big story.

The other thing we talked a lot about, which was so fitting for our crazy day, was how the wise men were probably very important and busy men. They were probably wealthy and had jobs, responsibilities, a family, and lots of things going on in their lives. And yet, when they saw the star appear in the sky, two things happened. First, they instantly knew it was a God sign. They knew without any doubt or hesitation that this star was a sign that their King had been born. How did they know that? How did they see it so quickly? I believe it is because they were looking. Even in the midst of their busy lives, they made time each day to look for signs of Jesus. How often do we get so busy that we forget to make time to look for Jesus in our lives?

The second thing the wise men did is that they went. Once they saw the star, they went to worship their king. It was not a close or short trip. It took them a long time. Riding on camels, at least that's what the story bibles say. Johnathan imagined that their butts must have gotten really sore and their backs would have been tired. I think he is probably right. It probably was not a convenient trip to make. Where were their families? What about their work and responsibilities at home? They literally saw a star in the sky and just left. Nothing in their important and busy lives was more important than them taking a gift to and going to worship their newborn King!

We discussed how hard it is for us to just make an impromptu trip to the grocery store. What if we were like the wise men, looking for signs of Christ in our everyday lives? Ready to jump up and go where ever He leads us at the drop of a hat. Of course this is a rather deep subject for a two-, four-, and five-year-old. I think I was talking to myself more than anything else. In the midst of my chaos, am I looking for signs from Jesus? Should my mayhem be an excuse to not seek Him and go when and where He leads? The answer to that last question is no, but so often we use it as an excuse to not spend that extra time in prayer talking with Him.

My lesson learned from this crazy, wild day: no excuses. Especially in scary times like these, we as Christians need to be on a constant lookout for signs of our Jesus. When we see those signs, because if we are looking we will see them, we need to be prepared for the task He entrusts us with. I believe that we are still here on this Earth, that He has not returned for us yet, because there is still work to do. There is still another child who needs to be saved. There is still another heart to be touched. There is still work to do for His Kingdom.

Sweet Father, thank you for today. Thank you for teaching me in the midst of the craziness to point my face to You. Help me, Jesus, to look for you each and every day. I want to be an obedient child of yours, waiting and watching for your instruction and your blessings. I pray that I might never hesitate to obey the callings you lay on my heart and in my path no matter how far away or difficult they may seem. The wise men traveled a huge and inconvenient distance to worship you, the least I can do is be an available vessel for your work. May my children see you through my obedience and may they come to have a God-seeking and obedient heart for You. Amen

Day 4

BEING ABOUT MY FATHER'S BUSINESS

This morning we found Elfie downstairs in our homeschool room surrounded by lots of friends. Woody, Buzz, Potato Head, Sven, the Smurfs, and the army guys were all there. It seemed he might have been trying to teach them something. We opened his bag and found our materials and Scripture lesson as usual.

> *And the child grew and became strong. He was very wise. He was blessed by God's grace. Every year Jesus' parents went to Jerusalem for the Passover Feast. When Jesus was 12 years old, they went up to the feast as usual. After the feast was over, his parents left to go back home. The boy Jesus stayed behind in Jerusalem. But they were not aware of it. They thought he was somewhere in their group. So they traveled on for a day. Then they began to look for him among their relatives and friends. They did not find him. So they went back to Jerusalem to look for him. After three days they found him in the temple courtyard. He was sitting with the*

teachers. He was listening to them and asking them questions. Everyone who heard him was amazed at how much he understood. They also were amazed at his answers. When his parents saw him, they were amazed. His mother said to him, "Son, why have you treated us like this? Your father and I have been worried about you. We have been looking for you everywhere."

"Why were you looking for me?" he asked. "Didn't you know I had to be in my Father's house?" But they did not understand what he meant by that.

Then he went back to Nazareth with them, and he obeyed them. But his mother kept all these things like a secret treasure in her heart. Jesus became wiser and stronger. He also became more and more pleasing to God and to people. (Luke 2:40–52)

This was an interesting story to read to the boys and discuss with them. While we painted our wooden Scripture ornament, our biggest topic of conversation was talking about what it would be like if one of them was separated from our family for three to four days. How scary that would be! Johnathan and Ian chatted about several stories and times that they almost got lost—at the grocery store or when they were running too far ahead of Mommy. Ian recalled one time recently when I said I was leaving. He had been lagging behind and not coming when he was asked. With all three boys in tow, I had lost the majority of my patience. If I had a third arm I would have picked him up to come but, alas, God chose to only give me two arms. I had said the classic mom line, "If you don't come right now I am going to leave. Bye-bye." Ian was not alarmed by my threats at this point so I shrugged my shoulders and walked with the other two boys around the corner where he could no longer see me. It did actually take him a few minutes but then it happened. "MOMMMMMY!" He came running down the aisle frantically looking for me, tears streaming down his cheeks. Recalling this "traumatic" event in his life, Ian said "Jesus must have been so afraid!"

The Bible tells us Jesus wasn't afraid at all. He was right there in the presence and company of His Father. As a mom I think about how Mary must have felt. Holy moly, I just lost the Messiah for four days! Seriously, you know she was in panic mode, right? When she finally finds Jesus, I can imagine her falling to her knees in front of him, grabbing him by both shoulders, looking at him at eye level. "Son, why have you done this? We were so afraid!" That's what any good mom would do, right? I have to be honest, I am so glad I am not Jesus's mom!

The next thing we talked about was Jesus's answer to his mother. He said in verse 49, "Why were you looking for me? Didn't you know I had to be in my Father's house?" Other translations say "Didn't you know I would be about my Father's business?" What does that answer mean? The passage tells us that Mary and Joseph did not understand what He meant. Now I am no Bible scholar, but my best answer to this question is that the temple should have been the first place they looked for Him because the temple was the house of God, His Father, and He was doing what God wanted Him to do. My question to the boys was, "If you were lost, where would the most logical place be for anyone to find you, and what would you be doing? Would it be a place that God would like you to be and something that He would like you to be doing?" Their answers were funny and sweet and I will just say, for now, I hope they don't get lost anytime soon!

As I reflected on my own questions, I began to wonder what my answers would be. When I am lost, separated from my community, where do I go first? Is it to my Father's house or is it to some other comfort of the world? Now I don't think for a minute that the twelve-year-old Jesus was afraid or was even lost for that matter. I believe that He knew His parents would be looking for Him and He knew the best place to go was the temple and the best thing for Him to be doing was to be around His Father's people doing His Father's work. So many times in our own lives we go through times where we feel lost or separated from those who are dear to us. I recently went through these feelings after we moved and I found myself without my wonderful church community. In the midst of this story I have heard a hundred times I found myself hearing a new lesson come out of this passage. When we feel lost, confused, unsure of where to go, the first place we should run is for the arms of Jesus and His people, the church. When we lose our sense of purpose, when we feel like we don't know what to do next, we should set out about our Father's work. Serve. When we serve we not only help others but we find ourselves in a community of other believers, family even. It is there inside that community that we grow in wisdom, and stature, and favor with God.

Are you lost today? Feeling alone and disconnected? I challenge you to find God's people and join them in their serving. Look around you and see where God is at work, and then join in!

Day 5

ELFIE GETS DUNKED

Today was a fun one to watch the boys discover. We found Elfie sitting in a pretend river. And by pretend river I really mean a clear container with a beach postcard taped to the side and some rocks in the bottom. What is he doing? I admit, my creative juices were a little off on this one.

> *Jesus came from Galilee to the Jordan River. He wanted to be baptized by John. But John tried to stop him. So he told Jesus, "I need to be baptized by you. So why do you come to me?"*
>
> *Jesus replied, "Let it be this way for now. It is right for us to do this. It carries out God's holy plan." Then John agreed.*
>
> *As soon as Jesus was baptized, he came up out of the water. At that moment heaven was opened. Jesus saw the Spirit of God coming down on him like a dove. A voice from heaven said, "This is my*

Son, and I love him. I am very pleased with him."
(Matthew 3:13–17)

This was an interesting topic to discuss as Johnathan accepted Christ as his savior several months ago, but we really have not talked with him a lot about what baptism is. To be honest, the boys had a hard time understanding why John didn't want to baptize Jesus at first. This one was tough to talk out in their young minds. Ultimately, what we settled upon understanding was that Jesus had to have someone baptize him and John was the person he wanted to do it. I know that may not be the best explanation, but for a four- and five-year-old, I think it is acceptable. We focused most on the "it carries out God's holy plan" part. We took some time to learn what baptism is and what it means. It is a symbol to God and others that you belong to Him. It is marking the moment where you belong to Christ and your sins are washed away, that you are a new creation in Him.

We imagined that we were down at the family's property on the New River and imagined what it would be like to see Jesus baptized there and the sky open up and a beautiful dove to come down. And then to hear the words, "This is my Son, and I love him. I am very pleased with him." Our ornament for the day was a simple dove we made to signify this event. My favorite part was acting this scene out a little bit. We put each of the boy's names, and my name, into the Scripture: "Jennifer is my daughter, and I love her. I am very pleased with her."

Can you imagine hearing God say that to you? How amazing! My first thought was, well, wouldn't that be awesome if that could be said of me. And then I caught myself . . .

Therefore, if anyone is in Christ, the new creation has come: The old has gone, the new is here! (2 Corinthians 5:17)

That *is* what God says about me! I am the one who says otherwise. The enemy is the one who wants me to believe that I am not wholly covered by the blood of Jesus. Am I worthy to be called that? No! The enemy is the one who would have me believe that my sin is too great and too vast to be covered by the cross. For me to believe such a lie is saying that Jesus's death on the cross was not good enough for me. Because of the cross, when God looks down at me He sees perfection. He sees His son's payment for me. This is what makes baptism so special. Baptism is the means by which I make a public profession of faith and discipleship. In the waters of baptism, I say, wordlessly, "I confess faith in Christ. Jesus has cleansed my soul from sin, and I now have a new life of dedication to God." Christian baptism illustrates the death, burial, and resurrection of Christ. At the same time, it also illustrates our death to sin and new life in Christ. As the sinner confesses to the Lord Jesus, he dies to sin (Romans 6:11) and is raised to a brand new life (Colossians 2:12). Being submerged in the water represents death to sin, and emerging from the water represents the cleansed, holy life that follows salvation. Romans 6:4 puts it this way: "We were therefore buried with him through baptism into death in order that, just as Christ was raised from the dead through the glory of the Father, we too may live a new life." Very simply, baptism is an outward testimony of the inward change in a believer's life.

Honestly, I think this lesson went over my boys' heads. And that's all right. They are young. But they are hearing it and every time they hear it that has to be a step in the right direction. And if nothing else, they are seeing their mom get excited remembering that she is a new creation in Christ! Get behind me, devil. You have no power over me. I am a child of the one true King of Heaven. I have been bought and paid for at a very high price. I am His beloved!

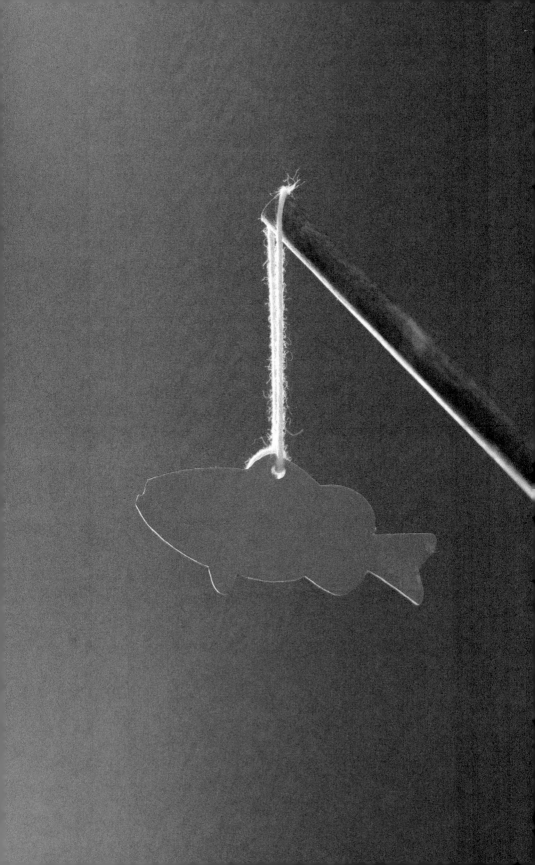

Day 6

GONE FISHIN'

think today was one of my favorite Elfie days! This morning we found Elfie sitting on the side of the hall bathroom sink with a fishing pole in his hand. Have you ever seen the kids fishing game with the little magnetic plastic fish that open and close their mouths on a turntable? Well, those are the fish Elfie was trying to catch in our sink!

One day Jesus was standing by the Sea of Galilee. The people crowded around him and listened to the word of God. Jesus saw two boats at the edge of the water. They had been left there by the fishermen, who were washing their nets. He got into the boat that belonged to Simon. Jesus asked him to go out a little way from shore. Then he sat down in the boat and taught the people.

When he finished speaking, he turned to Simon. Jesus said, "Go out into deep water. Let down the nets so you can catch some fish."

Simon answered, "Master, we've worked hard all night and haven't caught anything. But because you say so, I will let down the nets."

When they had done so, they caught a large number of fish. There were so many that their nets began to break. So they motioned to their partners in the other boat to come and help them. They came and filled both boats so full that they began to sink.

When Simon Peter saw this, he fell at Jesus' knees. "Go away from me, Lord!" he said. "I am a sinful man!" He and everyone with him were amazed at the number of fish they had caught. So were James and John, the sons of Zebedee, who worked with Simon.

Then Jesus said to Simon, "Don't be afraid. From now on you will fish for people." So they pulled their boats up on shore. Then they left everything and followed him. (Luke 5:1–11)

Our boys *love* to fish. One of their favorite things about our new home is that just around the corner there is a small stocked fishing pond. And by stocked I mean there are some nice big bass in there!

Whether in our little pond or down at the river property, we always have a good time fishing. I have even managed to get Ian brave enough to hook a worm! He is like his mom and enjoys sitting and watching the water, waiting for a bite. The other two boys are like their dad and are constantly reeling the line in and casting out again. Of course, Ian and I always catch more fish. So when the boys found Elfie doing a little fishing of his own, they were really excited. Our ornament today was a small wooden fish we decided to paint orange with white stripes, like Nemo, of course.

We talked about how frustrated Simon and the other fishermen must have been after fishing all night and without catching any fish. We are familiar with this frustration to an extent. I told the boys these men fished for a living so the fact that they hadn't caught anything was really bad for them. Johnathan said if he was Simon he would have rolled his eyes at Jesus for telling him to throw his nets back out. I love his honesty. Mostly because that is probably what most of us would have done, frustrated that this random dude thought he knew better than me about fishing. What a sight it must have been when the fish started pouring in! So many fish that the nets were tearing and the boats were sinking. Ian said that must have been fifty . . . ninety-nine . . . one hundred fish!

Our conversation turned a little toward trusting God when He tells us to do something. Trusting Him and obeying what He leads us to do as well. When we trust and obey, Jesus will always take care of us and bless us with more than we thought possible. And then came my favorite part of this story.

Jesus did something else really spectacular. He told the fishermen that if they followed Him, He would make them fishers of men. What did that mean? I wonder what the fishermen thought when He said that. They knew how to catch fish, but *men*? The Bible tells us that when we follow Jesus we also learn how to be "fishers of men." Instead of catching fish, we catch men. We tell people about Jesus so that they too want to follow Him! We talked about how they could talk to their friends about Jesus and that would make them fishermen for Jesus! They very much liked that idea . . . the gospel starting at a young age! I asked the boys, "What do you need to catch fish?" The boys responded that we would need a net or a fishing pole and of course some big worms. But what kind of bait do you use to catch men? They looked at me a little puzzled and took a minute to think about their answers. And then their answers just about made my heart burst! Ian said "Jesus!" And Johnathan followed, saying, "The Bible," I think those are pretty awesome answers!

We finished up the story talking about how the men responded to Jesus. How could they not follow a man who seemed to know everything? The fishermen left their boats and everything they had and followed Jesus. They became Jesus's disciples and learned from Jesus how to become "fishers of men." We decided this morning that we were going to talk to our friends about Jesus and His love for us.

In this life, we are going to be intentional about reaching others, just like the disciples were!

Our lesson tied in so well with our sermon this morning at church. I love it when God pulls things together for us! The big picture: A humble heart for others, by having the humble mind of Christ, will lead people to Jesus.

Just as an added tip: Fishing can be fun, but it can be a little messy and smelly. But when we catch men for Jesus, we don't have to clean them; Jesus takes care of that part.

Day 7

We found Elfie this morning perched high upon a tower. Ian was quite impressed at Elfie's building skills. He must have found our Widgets tote downstairs and boy did he make a tall tower! Our ornament parts were not in Elfie's bag but somehow Mommy had some extras lying around (aka I forgot to actually put them in the bag) and Mommy somehow knew what Scripture we were supposed to read! That Mommy sure is good! See, I told you I was not super mom.

> *Now when Jesus saw the crowds, he went up on a mountainside and sat down. His disciples came to him, and he began to teach them. He said:*
>
> *"Blessed are the poor in spirit, for theirs is the kingdom of heaven.*
>
> *"Blessed are those who mourn, for they will be comforted.*
>
> *"Blessed are the meek, for they will inherit the earth.*

"Blessed are those who hunger and thirst for righteousness, for they will be filled.

"Blessed are the merciful, for they will be shown mercy.

"Blessed are the pure in heart, for they will see God.

"Blessed are the peacemakers, for they will be called children of God.

"Blessed are those who are persecuted because of righteousness, for theirs is the kingdom of heaven.

"Blessed are you when people insult you, persecute you and falsely say all kinds of evil against you because of me. Rejoice and be glad, because great is your reward in heaven, for in the same way they persecuted the prophets who were before you.

"You are the salt of the earth. But if the salt loses its saltiness, how can it be made salty again? It is no longer good for anything, except to be thrown out and trampled underfoot.

"You are the light of the world. A town built on a hill cannot be hidden. Neither do people light a lamp and put it under a bowl. Instead they put it on its stand, and it gives light to everyone in the house. In the same way, let your light shine before others, that they may see your good deeds and glorify your Father in heaven. (Matthew 5:1–13)

This passage is a big bite to chomp off so we tried to break this passage down verse by verse to help the boys understand what Jesus was teaching the people about.

- Blessed are the poor in spirit—This is like us saying, "God, I am nothing without you. Please help me to be poor in spirit, humble, and depend on you for everything." Trying to explain "humble" to a four- and five-year-old was a bit challenging but I think they are beginning to understand

- Blessed are those who mourn—This one was fun if you have ever seen the movie *Inside Out*. In the movie Riley found joy through her mourning. When we hurt God by sinning, it should leave us heartbroken. In our home, if one of the boys says something mean, the other will often say, "You broke my heart!" We used this example to show how we should respond when we sin. We should have a broken heart, mourning, for what we have done to God. When this becomes our attitude of repentance, we will be blessed and comforted by God Almighty.

- Blessed are the meek—*Meek* means quiet, gentle, or submissive. Blessed are the ones who are gentle in their interactions with others and submissive to those they are to submit to.

- Blessed are those who hunger and thirst for righteousness—When we have a burning to do the right thing, to make God famous in our everyday lives, we will find the fullness of God.

- Blessed are the merciful—Taking out time of our day and resources to do things like helping at the food pantry and caring for others is being merciful. Realizing that we have so much that so many others do not have and go without. Being thankful for what we have and being merciful to others in the way that we help them and pray from them and sacrifice for them makes God happy.

- Blessed are the pure in heart—We need to be honest with others and honest with ourselves. We know what is right and wrong. And we know that when we choose to do wrong, we need to confess it and ask forgiveness. This makes Jesus happy and makes His home in our hearts much more comfy! (The last visualization compliments of Ian.)

- Blessed are the peacemakers—Honestly, we need more peacemakers in this house! We talked a lot about making peace with our brothers and friends even when we are wronged.
- Blessed are those who are persecuted for righteousness— This one was such an interesting one to talk to the boys about. With all of the scary times in our schools and communities with students and people being persecuted for their belief in Christ, there was something so rewarding to talk to our boys about never, ever backing down from their belief in God. No matter what you face, no matter if people laugh at you or harm you, you are a child of God. Your reward for always acknowledging Him will be found in heaven. Never, ever be ashamed of your Jesus! He was not ever ashamed of you!

We painted an ornament of a candle on an old-fashioned candle plate and talked about all of these things and how they were all ways that we could let our light shine for God. We sang some songs and got kind of silly acting some things out. At the end of the day, I sit here so proud of my boys. They are learning and learning to love a little more each day. Even though they don't even realize it yet, their lights are shinning so brightly. My prayer for us all today is that we never hide our light but let it shine brighter and brighter every day!

Day 8

CALMS THE STORM

This morning the boys had a tough time finding Elfie. They eventually, with a few hints, found him sailing in the Octonauts boat in their bathtub! What could he have been doing in there! Our craft for the day was to make a sailboat ornament to go along with our story. However, "Elfie" seems to have misplaced one of the pieces so our only materials were a small dowel and two felt sails. That naughty "Elfie." Okay, okay, I have absolutely no idea what happened to the main boat piece. It will turn up somewhere . . . maybe.

Jesus got into a boat. His disciples followed him. Suddenly a terrible storm came up on the lake. The waves crashed over the boat. But Jesus was sleeping. The disciples went and woke him up. They said, "Lord! Save us! We're going to drown!"

He replied, "Your faith is so small! Why are you so afraid?" Then Jesus got up and ordered the winds and the waves to stop. It became completely calm.

The disciples were amazed. They asked, "What kind of man is this? Even the winds and the waves obey him!" (Matthew 8:23–27)

Once we read this Johnathan started jumping up and down saying, "That's what Elfie was doing sleeping in the boat!" We took our materials and found a little wooden block and glued together a small sailboat ornament to remind of us this story. As we were waiting for the glue to dry, I asked the boys if they would be afraid like the disciples were. Naturally, since they are, of course, super heroes, their answers were "No, we wouldn't be afraid at all. Jesus is with us." *What?* Ha ha ha, these boys. From the mouths of babes, right! I confessed to them that I would be afraid but that they were correct. We should not be afraid when Jesus is with us. Next, I asked them if this story is the same type of thing we talk about when they are scared at night about having a bad dream. They are afraid sometimes about that, right? How could they be fearless in a boat at sea and yet afraid laying in their own beds at night? The mind of a kid, that's how. This hit closer to their reality. In the same way that the disciples should have had faith that Jesus would take care of them, Jesus is right here with us each day and night and we can have that same faith to trust Him to take care of us.

I think this is an important story and truth to remember for us adults in our daily routines and in hard times. What is going on in your life that is too big for God to handle? Trust God enough to give Him your stuff. He is big enough. He loves you enough. He has your best interest at heart. And He will never, ever fail!

Day 9

A HUNGRY ELFIE

This morning we came downstairs for breakfast and found our dear friend Elfie already grabbing a bite to eat ahead of us. He was sitting at the table with a plate full of marshmallows and chocolate chips. Much to the boys' dismay, Elfie's breakfast was not an acceptable breakfast for them to eat. I think if I would have chosen a better breakfast for Elfie our breakfast time would have been a little less whinny.

> *When Jesus came ashore, he saw a large crowd. He felt deep concern for them. He healed their sick people.*
>
> *When it was almost evening, the disciples came to him. "There is nothing here," they said. "It's already getting late. Send the crowds away. They can go and buy some food in the villages."*
>
> *Jesus replied, "They don't need to go away. You give them something to eat."*

"We have only five loaves of bread and two fish,"
they answered.

"Bring them here to me," he said. Then Jesus directed
the people to sit down on the grass. He took the five
loaves and the two fish. He looked up to heaven
and gave thanks. He broke the loaves into pieces.
Then he gave them to the disciples. And the disciples
gave them to the people. All of them ate and were
satisfied. The disciples picked up 12 baskets of left-
over pieces. The number of men who ate was about
5,000. Women and children also ate. (Matthew
14:14–21)

We had to read this story through about four times before it dawned on the boys that the story started with seven food items and ended with twelve baskets of leftovers. Johnathan looked at me quite puzzled. "Mommy, that doesn't make sense!" Johnathan, you are right, it doesn't make sense at all! How did that happen? We spent about fifteen or twenty minutes going back and forth about ways that they could break the pieces up so itty-bitty tiny and maybe that would fill twelve baskets. No matter how many ways we tried to wrap our heads around it, it just doesn't make sense. "That isn't good math," Johnathan said. This was such an awesome lesson in teaching them that when we give Jesus all that we have, He gives us so much more back in return.

It didn't make sense to the disciples either, but they obeyed anyway. Not only did Jesus make sure all the people were fed, but there was extra to spare! This is what we call a miracle—a surprising and welcome event that is not explicable by natural or scientific laws and is therefore considered to be the work of a divine agency (aka God).

Our ornament was a fish and bread loaf in a small basket and as we worked on painting it, we talked about other miracles that have happened in the world and in our lives. Like that one time that Mommy got a whole night of uninterrupted sleep . . . miracle. When Johnathan was in Mommy's tummy and was instantly healed from Vesa-Privea which doctors said would not correct itself . . . miracle.

The list could keep going on and on. Today I got to witness my boys realize what a miracle is. Seeing that awe and amazement in their eyes reminds me of how quickly we as grownups can take for granted what a miracle our life is. Do you have air in your lungs and a beating heart in your chest? A roof over your head and a book to read? Then you are so greatly blessed by our King! Today I pray that you will have a renewed and revitalized awe for the greatness and grace of our God!

Day 10

WALKING ON WATER

On the tenth day of our Christmas fun, we realized Elfie had rounded up all of our shoes and seemed to want to take a walk. Ian decided that he did not appreciate Elfie choosing his shoes to sit in, so now Ian is mad at Elfie. Oh the problems of a four-year-old.

Right away Jesus made the disciples get into the boat. He had them go on ahead of him to the other side of the Sea of Galilee. Then he sent the crowd away. After he had sent them away, he went up on a mountainside by himself to pray. Later that night, he was there alone. The boat was already a long way from land. It was being pounded by the waves because the wind was blowing against it.

Shortly before dawn, Jesus went out to the disciples. He walked on the lake. They saw him walking on the lake and were terrified. "It's a ghost!" they said. And they cried out in fear.

Right away Jesus called out to them, "Be brave! It is I. Don't be afraid."

"Lord, is it you?" Peter asked. "If it is, tell me to come to you on the water."

"Come," Jesus said.

So Peter got out of the boat. He walked on the water toward Jesus. But when Peter saw the wind, he was afraid. He began to sink. He cried out, "Lord! Save me!"

Right away Jesus reached out his hand and caught him. "Your faith is so small!" he said. "Why did you doubt me?"

When they climbed into the boat, the wind died down. Then those in the boat worshiped Jesus. They said, "You really are the Son of God!" (Mathew 14:22–33)

After I read this through the boys were like, "Okay, Mom, good story, are we done now?" I told them I didn't think they quite heard exactly what happened in the middle of the story, so I read it again. Still no reaction. I said, "Wow! Can you believe that He walked *on top* of the water?" Johnathan replied, "No, Mommy, He walked *in* the water to the boat." A-ha! Now I had them. I had to explain it a few more times while the boys tilted their heads and looked completely puzzled. "How did He do that?" asked Ian. Now that they understood that Jesus was walking *on* the water rather than *in* the water, they were intrigued. I asked them if they would be like Peter and if they would get out and walk to Jesus as well. Johnathan's reply was "Yes, I would, but I would never stop looking at Jesus because I don't want to go under the water and die!" Well, Johnathan, I think you have the right idea! Once the boys saw Jesus was big enough to walk on top of the water, they were sold. Why would you ever doubt someone who could walk on water? Why would you ever need to look away? Or want to, for that matter? Yet every day we do it so easily, naturally really. We have to actively and intentionally focus our eyes on Jesus in the midst of this crazy, stress-centered life.

I am learning so much through this study with my boys. Or maybe I should say that I am re-learning. These are all things that I have known, grew up knowing in Sunday school and church. But to hear them all again and teach them to my boys, to see the amazement in their eyes and hear their faith, is utterly overwhelming. I believe there is a reason that the Bible tells us to have childlike faith. Matthew 18 says:

> *Jesus called a little child over to him. He had the child stand among them. Jesus said, "What I'm about to tell you is true. You need to change and become like little children. If you don't, you will never enter the kingdom of heaven. Anyone who takes the humble position of this child is the most important in the kingdom of heaven.*

And one of my new favorites, Psalm 8:2, says:

> *You have made sure that children and infants praise you. Their praise is a wall that stops the talk of your enemies.*

Maybe today we all need to become a little more like the children that we care for. Maybe instead of brushing them off as an item on our to-do lists, or another stress to add to our day, maybe we should stop for a while and watch them . . . listen to them . . . teach them. For as we teach we will find ourselves learning so much more than we thought possible. The Bible gives us a great weapon to use against our enemy. Become like children, praise your God. Stop the talk of your enemies.

Day 11

LIKE A GOOD NEIGHBOR

Oh no! Elfie has lots of boo boos! What happened? We have to help him! These were the words coming from the boys this morning when they found Elfie laying on a pillow covered in Band-Aids. A little different from most mornings, for sure. Today was a lesson in what it means to love our neighbor.

> *One day an authority on the law stood up to test Jesus. "Teacher," he asked, "what must I do to receive eternal life?"*
>
> *"What is written in the Law?" Jesus replied. "How do you understand it?"*
>
> *He answered, "'Love the Lord your God with all your heart and with all your soul. Love him with all your strength and with all your mind.' [Deuteronomy 6:5] And, 'Love your neighbor as you love yourself.'" [Leviticus 19:18]*
>
> *"You have answered correctly," Jesus replied. "Do that, and you will live."*

But the man wanted to make himself look good. So he asked Jesus, "And who is my neighbor?"

Jesus replied, "A man was going down from Jerusalem to Jericho. Robbers attacked him. They stripped off his clothes and beat him. Then they went away, leaving him almost dead. A priest happened to be going down that same road. When he saw the man, he passed by on the other side. A Levite also came by. When he saw the man, he passed by on the other side too. But a Samaritan came to the place where the man was. When he saw the man, he felt sorry for him. He went to him, poured olive oil and wine on his wounds and bandaged them. Then he put the man on his own donkey. He brought him to an inn and took care of him. The next day he took out two silver coins. He gave them to the owner of the inn. 'Take care of him,' he said. 'When I return, I will pay you back for any extra expense you may have.'

"Which of the three do you think was a neighbor to the man who was attacked by robbers?"

The authority on the law replied, "The one who felt sorry for him."

Jesus told him, "Go and do as he did." (Luke 10:25–37)

To be honest, this one was pretty simple and self-explanatory. The boys knew very quickly who the good neighbor was and what the right thing to do was. There was no need for me to really add much. We made our ornament this morning which was a man with a bandage wrapped around his head. Johnathan was supposed to be painting brown hair on the little fella but he got a little excited and painted his whole head brown. He tried to wipe some off with a baby wipe and then just stared at him, shrugged his shoulders, and said,

"Well, maybe he was a brown person like Ms. Tanya." Don't you just love the honesty that kids possess?

We talked about how this story happened a long time ago, but there are people hurting all around us who need help. Johnathan was quick to recall a few times when we have been driving and stopped at a stoplight when someone would walk up to us with a sign asking for money. There are times I have rolled my window down and given some change and there are times I have looked the other way. Just being honest with you. We began discussing what those people might be doing on the street corner and why they might be there. The boys' response brought me to tears. They said, "Mommy, if they are hurting, then why don't we help them every time we see them? Don't we want to be like the Good Samaritan?" They are right. We could discuss at length the possibilities of how people arrive at certain places and what they might do with gifts given to them, but is that really the point? This Samaritan did not know the man he stopped to help or what that man's intentions were. He stopped because it is what God tells us to do . . . love. Isn't our God big enough to take care of the stewardship of that service to others? Wow, was I feeling some conviction!

So for part of our service this month we are going to make some care packages that we can give out to people we see on the street asking for help. They will have gloves, ChapStick, toothbrush, soap, deodorant, those types of things. This is just one way that we can be a "Good Samaritan" to our neighbors. I love that our boys are developing a heart for service! I can't wait to be able to take them on a mission trip and truly be able to do more with them!

My challenge to you today, how are you "loving your neighbor" this Christmas season? What could you do to touch the life of another that you aren't doing? I am not talking about money, I am talking about you giving a little of you. We can all do something to touch the life of another for the good.

Day 12

AN UNCLEAN DAY

This morning we discovered that Elfie has not only a naughty and humorous side, but also an artistic one! While we were sleeping he managed to turn all of our bananas into minions! One of my favorite things about the last twelve days is that Johnathan has been learning to look up the Scripture in his new Bible. We have really only been reading in Matthew and Luke, but Johnathan is now able to find those two books and locate the correct chapter and verses we are reading in! How awesome is that!

> *Jesus was on his way to Jerusalem. He traveled along the border between Samaria and Galilee. As he was going into a village, ten men met him. They had a skin disease. They were standing close by. And they called out in a loud voice, "Jesus! Master! Have pity on us!"*
>
> *Jesus saw them and said, "Go. Show yourselves to the priests." While they were on the way, they were healed.*

When one of them saw that he was healed, he came back. He praised God in a loud voice. He threw himself at Jesus' feet and thanked him. The man was a Samaritan.

Jesus asked, "Weren't all ten healed? Where are the other nine? Didn't anyone else return and give praise to God except this outsider?" Then Jesus said to him, "Get up and go. Your faith has healed you." (Luke 17:11–19)

I have heard so many sermons and teachings on this passage, all with different points and lessons. We put together and painted a red number ten as our ornament for this morning and then we focused on the fact that these ten sick men had no problem crying out to Jesus and asking Him for pity and healing. That is us, right? We don't think twice about crying out to God in our time of need and hardship. I think that is all right. Just like these men did, we believe that God has the power to heal us and it is good to look to Him for that healing. The second part of this story is that Jesus responded to the men. He gave them a simple instruction to "Go . . . show yourselves to the priest." Now I am confident that there is much to read into this instruction, but for the sake of preschool minds we are keeping it simple. They asked God for something, He asked them for something in return. Obedience. If we are going to seek God and beg mercy of Him, isn't it fair that we obey Him in return?

Of course the popular theme in this passage is that the men were all healed from their sickness on the way to the priest. They asked God for healing, they obeyed His instruction, they were healed. Awesome! That is a true miracle! The last part of this story, to me, is the most important. Only one man came back to give Jesus thanks. The Bible says he threw himself at the feet of Jesus. This is the proper response to being healed! He realized who his healer was and he wasted no time finding His feet. He didn't need to go running around showing people that he was better. He just needed to be in the presence of God Almighty. Why did the other men not return? What were they doing? Were they just "using" Jesus for their own personal gain? And the most important question, which man would we be? Would we be running to the feet of Jesus, throwing ourselves on our face before God in amazement and gratitude? Or would we be running around town, about our own business, forgetting the God who healed us? Now leave it to my sweet Ian to point out that this man was "at the feet of Jesus" and "I bet that was stinky!" You know, he is probably right! I love how naturally Ian thinks of these very practical parts of each story.

Of course the boys and I all agreed that we would be the man who went back to thank Jesus, but I can't help but wonder how often in our daily lives we forget about the God who has healed us or rescued us from a wreck we might have been in, or the God who wakes us up each day with air in our lungs and a beating heart in our chest. If I am honest, I think most days I am more like the nine men who never returned than I am the one man falling at the feet of Jesus. I don't want to be one of those nine men, but if I do not live my life on purpose I can get so caught up in *my* agenda and what I did today.

Father, help us to be constantly living at your feet. Help us to be ever mindful of every second that you bless us and give us so much more than we deserve. At Your "stinky" feet is where I want to live every moment, every day.

Day 13

THE IMPORTANCE OF ONE

This morning we came downstairs to find Elfie hiding around the corner on a "huge" tower of red solo cups. These cups proceeded to be dramatically knocked down and stomped on by the youngest Moye boy, to which the older two started screaming and crying that he made Elfie fall. Perfect way to start a Sunday morning, right? We didn't get around to doing our story and craft until this evening since Sunday mornings are a wild storm of emotions, baths, hating dress clothes, and trying to get out the door in time. Is it that way in anybody else's house? If so, find comfort in knowing you are not alone.

> The tax collectors and sinners were all gathering around to hear Jesus. But the Pharisees and the teachers of the law were whispering among themselves. They said, "This man welcomes sinners and eats with them." Then Jesus told them a story. He said, "Suppose one of you has 100 sheep and loses one of them. Won't he leave the 99 in the open country? Won't he go and look for the one lost sheep until

he finds it? When he finds it, he will joyfully put it on his shoulders and go home. Then he will call his friends and neighbors together. He will say, 'Be joyful with me. I have found my lost sheep.' I tell you, it will be the same in heaven. There will be great joy when one sinner turns away from sin. Yes, there will be more joy than for 99 godly people who do not need to turn away from their sins.

"Or suppose a woman has ten silver coins and loses one. Won't she light a lamp and sweep the house? Won't she search carefully until she finds the coin? And when she finds it, she will call her friends and neighbors together. She will say, 'Be joyful with me. I have found my lost coin.' I tell you, it is the same in heaven. There is joy in heaven over one sinner who turns away from sin." (Luke 15)

This story was fun to talk about with the boys. We took out the white paint and cotton balls and painted a small sheep ornament while we talked about the realization that when Johnathan accepted Christ into his heart a few months ago, heaven had a rockin' party! He really liked this image. We talked a bit about how each time that someone turns from their sin and turns toward Jesus the angels do a "happy dance." We got up and danced around like we thought the angels might be doing. We talked about celebrating this way when one of our friends or family accepts Jesus into their heart. We related back to the story a few days ago about baptism and talked about how when people get baptized we should all be dancing in our pews in joy for their commitment. The boys imagined that there must be a lot of partying in heaven. Fun place to be, huh?

We spend so much time as parents teaching our kids that it is better to think of others and give to others. We spend a lot of time trying to instill in them a servant's heart and a passion for other people. Honestly, I believe this story is about the power of one. One sheep, one person . . . us. If I was that one lost sheep Jesus would come for me and go through everything He went through even if it was just for my single soul. In the same way, it is about you. It's about our lost friend from playgroup. It's about our coworker, the lady who makes our coffee, the server at lunch, the cop who pulls you over, the next door neighbor. It's about all of us and at the same time about just one. What I want the boys to walk away knowing, and what I want you to know, is that they are so deeply important to the God of the universe that He would leave everything to come to their rescue. We are all that important, that loved. Do I want them to be focused on others and self-sacrificing and humble? Of course. I also want them to grasp the awe that they are loved by their Maker in a never-ending, all-consuming, unconditional kind of way. I want them to wake up, brush their teeth, eat their Cheerios, play, and sleep right here in the presence of God Almighty every day with His love living in the air we breathe. I want them to know how important each life is. I want them to be so encompassed by the Holy Spirit that when they find themselves outside of the covering of God's love, in a dark place where sin abides, they would literally shudder from feeling His absence. They will find themselves in those places in life, it is inevitable. When they do, I want them to know without doubt who they are and whose they are. Because they know that love so confidently, because they know who they are, then they will know what to do. When we understand our value, our identity in Christ, what confidence and strength there is to be found!

Growing up my dad did not really set a lot of rules for me if I was going out with friends. He would usually tell me one thing on my way out the door: "Remember who you are and whose you are." Even into adulthood this saying has stayed with me and translated into so many areas of my life. As I have grown, and continue to do so, there are times in life when it is hard to see who I am. Am I Mom? Wife? Friend? Servant? Slave? Employee? Does anyone really care? Who am I? This passage reminds me today that I am a cherished and valued child of the King. I am worth everything to Him and I am His. He loves me with an unfailing love. He tells me over and over again through Scripture who I am, all I need to do is listen and focus on Him. I need to believe He is who He says He is, and because of that truth then I am who He says I am. I am who He says I am . . . and so are you!

Day 14

WALK THIS WAY

Apparently little Elfie got a bit hungry last night! We found him this morning in our cookie barn and he had made quite a mess! Ian says I should spank his bottom. Johnathan was excited to eat Elfie's crumbs but soon discovered they were there because they were a trial batch of Mom's gluten-free cookies that didn't turn out so well. Sorry to disappoint, Johnathan. Again, not super mom.

> *A few days later, Jesus entered Capernaum again. The people heard that he had come home. So many people gathered that there was no room left. There was not even room outside the door. And Jesus preached the word to them. Four of those who came were carrying a man who could not walk. But they could not get him close to Jesus because of the crowd. So they made a hole by digging through the roof above Jesus. Then they lowered the man through it on a mat. Jesus saw their faith. So he said to the man, "Son, your sins are forgiven."*

Some teachers of the law were sitting there. They were thinking, "Why is this fellow talking like that? He's saying a very evil thing! Only God can forgive sins!"

Right away Jesus knew what they were thinking. So he said to them, "Why are you thinking these things? Is it easier to say to this man, 'Your sins are forgiven'? Or to say, 'Get up, take your mat and walk'? But I want you to know that the Son of Man has authority on earth to forgive sins." So Jesus spoke to the man who could not walk. "I tell you," he said, "get up. Take your mat and go home." The man got up and took his mat. Then he walked away while everyone watched. All the people were amazed. They praised God and said, "We have never seen anything like this!" (Mark 2)

Of course our ornament went along with the story as we painted the little man and made a stretcher for him out of little sticks and scrap fabric. Johnathan was familiar with this story, but Ian was hearing it for the first time and could not believe that they made a hole in the roof! We imagined how crowded the house must have been that the only way they could get to Jesus was through the roof. I asked the boys if they were surprised that Jesus healed the man and made him able to walk again. "Nope," they said with a matter-of-fact look. "He's Jesus, He can do whatever He wants to do." So obviously by day fourteen they are beginning to understand Jesus a little bit, right? We talked about how time after time in the Bible we read stories about how people did not believe Jesus was who He said He was. They doubted Him until He performed some type of miracle and then they were always so amazed. Johnathan put his hands on his hips and tilted his head sideways. "Why do they do that? Don't they know who He is?" I love his spirit!

It is easy to read the stories and ask those questions today because we have the Bible to read and know God's Word. Back then the people didn't have the Bible. They had never heard of Jesus before so if we pretend to be them we would probably be very skeptical too! In fact, I think even today when a miracle happens or when God answers someone's prayer we are often so surprised! Should we be surprised when God does what He says He will do? When we pray, are we praying expecting God to actually answer our prayers?

This man must have had some pretty awesome friends! They went to some pretty extreme measure to get their friend in front of Jesus because they knew and trusted that Jesus would answer their prayers. They went to that house expectant. I wasn't there, but I bet those friends were not surprised at all that their friend got up and walked out. I bet the just smiled and rejoiced with him. We talked about whether we would do something like that for our friends if they needed it. Would we go out of our way to help a friend like that? What if that man didn't have those friends? Would he have ever walked again? The role of our Christian friends and family is such an important part of life. We are meant to live in community so that we can share each other's burdens. So that when one of us is down or hurt, the others will carry us to the feet of Jesus no matter the obstacle.

Father, I pray that my boys will grow to be friends like this man had. I pray that they will be stretcher carriers for others and that when hard times come they will know to find You first. I pray that I would be the same. May we seek You and pray expecting You to do what You say You will do. And may we never lose the awe of Your greatness!

After our lesson we went with some other friends to visit an assisted living home near us and sing some Christmas carols. This is the first time our boys had ever been in a nursing home type of environment so I wasn't sure how they would respond. After all, they are boys! Thankfully they did really well. Johnathan worked a puzzle with one of the ladies and I think that was such a blessing to her. He and Ian joined in the singing with their friends and then handed out candy canes to the residents. Jacob . . . he did not want to be there. Just being honest. I wrestled with him the entire time and I believe that he interrupted the singing with screams at least half a dozen times. But hey, that's life, right? I don't think the boys realized the blessing their sweet voices and actions were to the women there but you could see on those wise faces smiles of joy. Last night we watched the movie *Elf*, so the boys' favorite quote for the day was "The best way to spread Christmas cheer is singing loud for all to hear."

Day 15

QUENCHING A THIRST

What a strange place we found Elfie in this morning! He was tucked up in the water and ice dispenser of the refrigerator as if he was getting a nice cold drink of water. The boys found this to be particularly funny this morning and they cackled over him for at least fifteen to twenty minutes.

> *He came to a town in Samaria called Sychar. It was near the piece of land Jacob had given his son Joseph. Jacob's well was there. Jesus was tired from the journey. So he sat down by the well. It was about noon.*
>
> *A woman from Samaria came to get some water. Jesus said to her, "Will you give me a drink?" His disciples had gone into the town to buy food.*
>
> *The Samaritan woman said to him, "You are a Jew. I am a Samaritan woman. How can you ask me for a drink?" She said this because Jews don't have anything to do with Samaritans.*

Jesus answered her, "You do not know what God's gift is. And you do not know who is asking you for a drink. If you did, you would have asked him. He would have given you living water."

"Sir," the woman said, "you don't have anything to get water with. The well is deep. Where can you get this living water? Our father Jacob gave us the well. He drank from it himself. So did his sons and his livestock. Are you more important than he is?"

Jesus answered, "Everyone who drinks this water will be thirsty again. But anyone who drinks the water I give them will never be thirsty. In fact, the water I give them will become a spring of water in them. It will flow up into eternal life."

The woman said to him, "Sir, give me this water. Then I will never be thirsty. And I won't have to keep coming here to get water."

He told her, "Go. Get your husband and come back."

"I have no husband," she replied.

Jesus said to her, "You are right when you say you have no husband. The fact is, you have had five husbands. And the man you live with now is not your husband. What you have just said is very true."

"Sir," the woman said, "I can see that you are a prophet. Our people have always worshiped on this mountain. But you Jews claim that the place where we must worship is in Jerusalem."

Jesus said, "Woman, believe me. A time is coming when you will not worship the Father on this mountain or in Jerusalem. You Samaritans worship what you do not know. We worship what we do know.

Salvation comes from the Jews. But a new time is coming. In fact, it is already here. True worshipers will worship the Father in the Spirit and in truth. They are the kind of worshipers the Father is looking for. God is spirit. His worshipers must worship him in the Spirit and in truth."

The woman said, "I know that Messiah is coming." Messiah means Christ. "When he comes, he will explain everything to us."

Then Jesus said, "The one you're talking about is the one speaking to you. I am he."

Just then Jesus' disciples returned. They were surprised to find him talking with a woman. But no one asked, "What do you want from her?" No one asked, "Why are you talking with her?"

The woman left her water jar and went back to the town. She said to the people, "Come. See a man who told me everything I've ever done. Could this be the Messiah?" The people came out of the town and made their way toward Jesus. (John 4)

This one was a little tough to keep the boys' attention spans on since it was a bit of a longer passage than what we have been reading, so we painted our water bucket ornament while I read through the passage. My next challenge came from deciding which lesson I wanted them to walk away with from this story. There are so many different ways to look at this and directions to learn from. We decided to talk about two parts of the story for time and attention's sake. The first was that Jesus met this lady and He asked her for a drink from the well. The first really cool thing is that even though He had never met her, He knew everything about her. He knew that she had five husbands and that she was living with a man out of wedlock currently. First off, God knows everything about us. Even the things we don't want Him to know! I asked the boys if it scared them that there were no secrets from Jesus. Of course at their age they don't have many skeletons in their closets, yet. For us grownups, this can really be a scary thing, right? I am sure this lady wasn't proud of her situation and probably didn't really care for others to know all about it. My favorite part is that Jesus knows all her dirty laundry, and He loved her despite it. Jesus knows us better than anyone else ever could, even better than Mommy and Daddy! No matter what we do or say or where we come from or how far we stray from Him, He still loves us.

Next I attempted to explain to the boys what Jesus meant when He said that He could give her "living water." To be honest with you, I think I explained this five times and I received blank stares in return. So we settled for living water meaning that when we take Jesus in our hearts, as in drinking living water, we receive eternal life with Him. Sounds about right, right?

Finally, Jesus and the woman talk about where they are to worship. Now my boys have a mom who loves to sing so they knew the answer to this one right away. "We worship everywhere!" was their answer. Insert big mommy smile. I asked them what type of places we worship in. They had answers like, "In the van," "At church," "Bath time," "In the school room," "While Mommy is cooking," you get the idea. Jesus was telling this woman it does not matter where a person worships or what they call themselves. It only matters how they worship. Your worship must be spiritual, genuine, real.

All this talk about living waters got me humming a '90s tune in my head by the Gather Vocal Band

> *Have you ever walked through a burnin' dusty desert*
>
> *Where the sun beats down and scorches your soul?*
>
> *And have you ever knelt and prayed to God for mercy*
>
> *'Cause you don't know how much farther you can go?*
>
> *Well, there's a place of rest just over that horizon.*

When I'm tired and thirsty, that's where I go.

All I really need is a taste of that refreshing

From the spring of life where living water flows,

I'm goin' back to the source of living water.

That abundant supply will never run dry.

When I get to feelin' dry and thirsty down in my soul,

I just go back to where the living water flows.

On the road of life, sometimes I get discouraged,

And I start to wonder if I've lost my way.

Did I make the right decision at the crossroads,

Or should I take the road that's better paved?

Well, then I hear the sound of cool, clear rushing water

Like a mountain stream runnin' right through my soul,

And I know that ev'ry mile has been rewarded

By the cup of living water that I hold.

Day 16

BRING AN OFFERING

This morning Elfie was sitting in our Christmas tree, the same place he was last night when we went to bed. That's right, I forgot to move him. I will say it again, no super mom here. Thankfully the boys made up their own reasoning for him being in the tree instead of some naughty place. They said, "Look, Mom, Elfie was good last night. Maybe he is learning something from us!" Mom score!

> *Jesus sat down across from the place where people put their temple offerings. He watched the crowd putting their money into the offering boxes. Many rich people threw large amounts into them. But a poor widow came and put in two very small copper coins. They were worth only a few pennies.*
>
> *Jesus asked his disciples to come to him. He said, "What I'm about to tell you is true. That poor widow has put more into the offering box than all the others. They all gave a lot because they are rich. But she gave even though she is poor. She put in everything she had. That was all she had to live on." (Mark 12:41–44)*

Today was a great lesson for our sweet Johnathan. He has been working very hard to save up some of his money from doing chores and winning nickels from Grandpa but today was the first time he was introduced to tithing. Our ornament was a little bag with two plastic coins which reminded the boys of Chuck-E-Cheese coins.

What are offerings? A shrug of the shoulders is the response I got. Sigh, it's one of those mornings. An offering is a gift you give to someone. Why do people give offerings at the church? "To pay for things," Johnathan answered. Well, yes, it is to pay for things. More importantly, we give an offering out of obedience to what God has told us to do. We continued to talk on about how blessed we are and that God is the one who gives to us and allows us to have all the wonderful things and the money that we have. When we become Christians, we become God's property. We are His children and all that we have is really His. He is merely allowing us to use it while we are here living on earth. Johnathan was kind of following me on this, so we continued. Why do you think Jesus told His disciples that the poor woman's two coins was a greater offering than the rich people's offerings? He had no idea, and I didn't expect him to. We talked about how it doesn't matter if we give God $1,000 or $1, what matters is that we trust Him enough to give Him what He asks for and what we have. The poor woman gave everything that she had because she trusted God and was obedient in giving to Him. The rich men gave a lot of money, but they still had lots of money to live on. A true offering requires sacrifice. It will cost us something. It sometimes means we have to go without something we really want. But, when we are obedient and happy givers, God always blesses us way more in return!

This was a natural lead-in to be able to talk with Johnathan about tithing. We have always tithed as a family and wholeheartedly believe it is what God instructs us to do. Even as a kid I can remember my parents being much like this poor woman, putting in the last dollars they had, trusting that God would provide. And He always did and still does! I asked Johnathan to go get his little wallet where he keeps all his treasures. He jumped up and was proud to sit down and count out all his money with me. I am so proud at what a good little saver he is. Just like his daddy. Yep, that's right, he didn't get the saving gene from me.

We got out some construction paper and tape and an old Tupperware bowl and made our own little tithing jar. Johnathan had about $8 saved up in his wallet. I told him that in the Bible God instructs us that we should tithe one-tenth of what money we bring in. We counted out ten pennies and I showed him that one-tenth of those ten would be one penny. He was following along and nodding his head. I told him that as he is getting older and starting to make a little money with the extra chores he does for Mommy and the gifts he gets from family, that Jesus has asked him to start tithing. One-tenth of the money he has. Now Johnathan started looking worried. I helped him and we decided that 80 cents would be one-tenth of the $8 he had. So we counted out three quarters and five pennies, 80 cents. Then I asked him, "Okay, what has Jesus asked you to do with that 80 cents?" He looked at me with a sad face and pointed to the tithing jar. I have to admit it was hard not to laugh at his honesty. If we were all honest, you know you have felt this way about tithing before. I know I have. It's my money. I worked hard for it. I need my stuff.

I reminded Johnathan that everything we have, even our money, comes from God. Look around us at how blessed we are. God doesn't need your 80 cents, Johnathan. He really doesn't. He is God. He doesn't need anyone's money. Tithing is an act of obedience and faith. It shows God that you know the money is His to begin with and you are only borrowing it. It shows God that you trust Him. It shows God that you love Him enough to do what He asks of you. It is such a small service in comparison to the rewards and blessings and love that God gives us. Johnathan, Jesus wants you to give, and He wants you to give with a joyful heart knowing that by giving Him that 80 cents you are putting a great big smile on the face of God! Johnathan's sad face turned to a happy one and he dropped his 80 cents into the jar with a bounce of excitement.

What an inspiring reminder that we are to be joyful givers, not reluctant ones. God doesn't need our money to fulfill His plans, He is God. What He requires is our obedience. John 14:21 says, "If you love me you will obey my teachings."

So, my five-year-old son is tithing. Are you?

Day 17

MY TOES HURT

Today we found out sweet little Elfie making some tasty snow angels in Mommy's baking stuff. That naughty guy had dumped a pile of powdered sugar all over our kitchen island!

Jesus and his disciples went on their way. Jesus came to a village where a woman named Martha lived. She welcomed him into her home. She had a sister named Mary. Mary sat at the Lord's feet listening to what he said. But Martha was busy with all the things that had to be done. She came to Jesus and said, "Lord, my sister has left me to do the work by myself. Don't you care? Tell her to help me!"

"Martha, Martha," the Lord answered. "You are worried and upset about many things. But few things are needed. Really, only one thing is needed. Mary has chosen what is better. And it will not be taken away from her." (Luke 10:38–42)

I am not going to lie, I really wanted to skip this day. There are so many other things in the Bible to learn about, right? We don't really need to do this lesson today, do we? I mean, really?

If you know me, you know that I struggle with being more like Mary and less like Martha. I think if we are honest we would say a lot of us have this struggle, especially us moms.

As we read through the story we talked about what it would be like if Jesus came to our house to visit. Like really knocked on the door as a "normal" person and sat down on our crumb-filled couch and had a cheese sandwich with us. We laughed and giggled at what He would find in our house. Mostly the mess. Just talking about it with them made me want to start cleaning! Then my very wise five-year-old said, "But, Mommy, Jesus is here in our house with us all the time. That's what you told me. And He is in our hearts. So He already sees our mess."

Enough said. Drop-the-microphone moment. Yes, my boy, you are so right! Jesus is here in our house with us! And He is everywhere we are. He knows all about us and what we focus on the most. In this story, Martha was rushing around trying to clean up the mess, and make great food, and be an amazing hostess for her very important guest. There is nothing wrong with what she was doing. Don't miss the point here. When Martha asks Jesus to make Mary help her, Jesus doesn't scold Martha for trying to care for Him. He simply says, "Baby girl, I love your heart of service. But Mary is doing what is best. I am best. Being still in my presence and listening to my words are the most important. Hear my voice, focus on me. Let me take care of the mess." (My words, not His.)

Since I was talking to a four- and five-year-old, we talked mostly about making God the most important focus of our day. He is always watching us and He wants us to think of Him first in our day. In this story of Jesus visiting Martha and Mary, we are reminded that Jesus wants us to look to Him before anything or anyone else, yet our lives are full of distractions that get in the way of making him our number one priority.

Our ornament was a simple rolling pin to symbolize the work we can get caught up in every day. Ironic, since I love to bake and all.

What a great reminder as we come up on Christmas and New Year to truly focus on the miracle that He is. It is so easy to get caught up in the hustle of life, changing diapers, hosting people, keeping up, cooking, cleaning, trying to be super mom, and such that we don't spend the time to just be still and sit down at the feet of Jesus. My challenge to you today is both simple and complex. Take some time today and be still, sitting in awe at the feet of our Heavenly Father.

Day 18

A TRIUMPHAL ENTRY

Elfie must have been missing the North Pole this morning as we found him bundled up with a kitchen towel in the fridge. It was fun watching the boys run around the house trying to find him. They only found him in the fridge when they went to get a drink.

> As they all approached Jerusalem, they came to Bethphage. It was on the Mount of Olives. Jesus sent out two disciples. He said to them, "Go to the village ahead of you. As soon as you get there, you will find a donkey tied up. Her colt will be with her. Untie them and bring them to me. If anyone says anything to you, say that the Lord needs them. The owner will send them right away."

> This took place so that what was spoken through the prophet would come true. It says,

> "Say to the city of Zion,

> 'See, your king comes to you.

He is gentle and riding on a donkey.

He is riding on a donkey's colt.'" [Zechariah 9:9]

The disciples went and did what Jesus told them to do. They brought the donkey and the colt. They placed their coats on them for Jesus to sit on. A very large crowd spread their coats on the road. Others cut branches from the trees and spread them on the road. Some of the people went ahead of him, and some followed. They all shouted,

"Hosanna to the Son of David!

"Blessed is the one who comes in the name of the Lord!" [Psalm 118:26]

"Hosanna in the highest heaven!"

When Jesus entered Jerusalem, the whole city was stirred up. The people asked, "Who is this?"

The crowds answered, "This is Jesus. He is the prophet from Nazareth in Galilee."

Jesus entered the temple courtyard. He began to drive out all those who were buying and selling there. He turned over the tables of the people who were exchanging money. He also turned over the benches of those who were selling doves. He said to them, "It is written that the Lord said, 'My house will be called a house where people can pray.' [Isaiah 56:7] But you are making it 'a den for robbers.'" [Jeremiah 7:11] (Mathew 21)

Our craft was to paint a donkey ornament which was super fun to do as we talked about Jesus being in a parade as He came into Jerusalem. We laid down our coats and pillows onto the floor in the living room and took turns walking over them doing the "queen wave." Probably not exactly how it really happened but they got the idea. People were celebrating and welcoming Jesus, calling him Hosanna.

Once Jesus came into the city He went straight to the temple. What He found there were people gambling and selling things. They had made the place of worship into a flea market. What do we go to the church building to do? The boys quickly answered, "To worship and learn about Jesus." Absolutely! Now there are many things that happen at church, but the main reason for having a church building, a temple, is to worship God corporate! Further, Jesus says, "My house will be a house where people can pray." Could the people pray and worship God very well when others were selling things and exchanging money? No. That would be like trying to worship in the mall.

We talk a lot in our house about controlling our anger and our emotions. I knew this one would be a tough one to explain without the boys feeling like they could start turning over tables when they got mad.

Were Jesus's actions appropriate? Is there any time when we would be authorized to use such behavior in God's behalf? While we always look to Jesus as a pattern for our behavior, we must remember that Jesus was God's son. The temple was God's house, the home of Jesus's father. Jesus had authority there. He had the right to chase unwanted cheaters out of his father's house. It was his house too. Just as Mommy and Daddy have the right to ask misbehaving guests to leave our home, Jesus had the authority to eject people from His father's house. His actions were based on His position, which is exactly what the Pharisees and others were challenging him on. They asked him what authority did He have. He had it all, but as we will see in the next few days, they would not believe.

Day 19

WASHING ANOTHER'S FEET

We keep finding Elfie in the silliest places. I got so tickled at the boys this morning as they searched and searched for Elfie and he was right there hiding in plain sight. He had climbed up on the cabinets and wrapped himself up in the Christmas decorations. I guess he might have blended in with the cabinet decorations more than I thought.

> When the hour came, Jesus and his apostles took their places at the table. He said to them, "I have really looked forward to eating this Passover meal with you. I wanted to do this before I suffer. I tell you, I will not eat the Passover meal again until it is celebrated in God's kingdom."
>
> After Jesus took the cup, he gave thanks. He said, "Take this cup and share it among yourselves. I tell you, I will not drink wine with you again until God's kingdom comes."

Then Jesus took bread. He gave thanks and broke it. He handed it to them and said, "This is my body. It is given for you. Every time you eat it, do this in memory of me."

In the same way, after the supper he took the cup. He said, "This cup is the new covenant in my blood. It is poured out for you. (Luke 22:14–20)

So he got up from the meal and took off his outer clothes. He wrapped a towel around his waist. After that, he poured water into a large bowl. Then he began to wash his disciples' feet. He dried them with the towel that was wrapped around him.

He came to Simon Peter. "Lord," Peter said to him, "are you going to wash my feet?"

Jesus replied, "You don't realize now what I am doing. But later you will understand."

"No," said Peter. "You will never wash my feet."

Jesus answered, "Unless I wash you, you can't share life with me."

"Lord," Simon Peter replied, "not just my feet! Wash my hands and my head too!"

Jesus answered, "People who have had a bath need to wash only their feet. The rest of their body is clean. And you are clean. But not all of you are." Jesus knew who was going to hand him over to his enemies. That was why he said not everyone was clean.

When Jesus finished washing their feet, he put on his clothes. Then he returned to his place. "Do you understand what I have done for you?" he asked them. "You call me 'Teacher' and 'Lord.' You are right. That is what I am. I, your Lord and Teacher, have washed your feet. So you also should wash one

another's feet. I have given you an example. You
should do as I have done for you. (John 13:4–15)

The first part of this story tells us of the Last Supper and what we today call as communion. We took out a piece of bread and some juice. I broke the bread in half and we talked about what it might have been like to be at that table. We talked about what it meant to symbolize the bread as Jesus's body and the juice His blood. Jesus told the disciples this would be His last meal with them. We imagined they were probably worried and sad since they loved Jesus so much.

Then Jesus did something so unexpected. He gets down on His knees and washes the dirty feet of the disciples. Jesus tells Peter that he must allow Him to wash his feet if he wanted to share life with Him. I love Peter's response. Wash everything! We talked about how Jesus did this as an example of how we are to serve others. This was His final instruction to the disciples before He went to the cross. The most important thing He wanted them to remember. Serve as I have served you.

We have talked a lot this month about serving others and showing God's love to people everywhere. As we were painting a small water pitcher and bowl for our ornament, Ian made me smile when he commented, "Mommy, you wash our feet and our whole bodies when we take a bath. You are just like Jesus!" I love his confidence in me. I am nowhere near being like Jesus, but I love that the boys got the lesson. Ian made me realize something so very important. I do serve them by washing them. The care I give my family is not unnoticed and unimportant. I am serving them…like Jesus.

Day 20

A STROLL IN THE GARDEN

This morning we found Elfie swinging like Tarzan through the Christmas lights on a candy cane. I thought the boys would really be impressed with this Elfie appearance but instead they just wanted to fight over who got to eat his candy cane.

> Then Jesus went with his disciples to a place called Gethsemane. He said to them, "Sit here while I go over there and pray." He took Peter and the two sons of Zebedee along with him. He began to be sad and troubled. Then he said to them, "My soul is very sad. I feel close to death. Stay here. Keep watch with me."
>
> He went a little farther. Then he fell with his face to the ground. He prayed, "My Father, if it is possible, take this cup of suffering away from me. But let what you want be done, not what I want."
>
> Then he returned to his disciples and found them sleeping. "Couldn't you men keep watch with me for one hour?" he asked Peter. "Watch and pray. Then

you won't fall into sin when you are tempted. The spirit is willing, but the body is weak."

Jesus went away a second time. He prayed, "My Father, is it possible for this cup to be taken away? But if I must drink it, may what you want be done."

Then he came back. Again he found them sleeping. They couldn't keep their eyes open. So he left them and went away once more. For the third time he prayed the same thing.

Then he returned to the disciples. He said to them, "Are you still sleeping and resting? Look! The hour has come. The Son of Man is about to be handed over to sinners. (Matthew 26:36–45)

Can you imagine going to a garden with Jesus and Him telling you He feels close to death? He instructs you to keep lookout with Him. You can tell He is very troubled. And yet you fall asleep . . . three times! I would hate to be those guys!

Unfortunately, I think all too often we are just like those men. God instructs us to do something, sometimes a hard thing and sometimes just little things, and we just sit there and sleep.

I love this passage because it so simply reveals the humanness of Jesus. He doesn't want to feel the pain that He knows is coming. He asks His father three times to please take it from Him. But He also prays that God's will would be done. If there is any way. I think this is such a wonderful example of how we should pray in times of suffering. I have been praying a lot lately for my grandparents. My grandfather has some medical issues and it is just heartbreaking to see it taking over their lives. I want to pray that God would just heal him and let him live out the rest of his days enjoying his wife and grandkids. He has served God with much of his life, doesn't God owe him that? And then I realize how selfish my prayer is. Not just for me but for him as well. When I read of Jesus's example here I find that my prayer should be, "Father, if you can take the suffering away and still accomplish your plans for him, please do so. If not, I pray that you would make his suffering a shining light to others, guiding them to you. I pray that his days will be filled with service to others and to You. And that You would give him his daily portion to get through each day. I pray that his mind will be focused on You and not the pain. I pray that his family will see Your amazing face through all that he does. I pray that his family that does not know You. I pray that they will come to know You through his life. And when Your work is complete for him, I pray that You will take him home to be with You and crown him with the many crowns he deserves. I can't wait to see him dancing the streets of heaven with You and know that he is kneeling forevermore at his Savior's precious feet." That's what I should pray . . . and from now on that will be my prayer.

I think we are all here until God's work with us is complete. I often hear people saying, "I'm just waiting for the Lord to bring me home." While I understand fully the longing to be united with our Heavenly Father, it just gets under my skin when I hear this. It's just like my first prayer—selfish. *We* want to go to heaven. If God was done with us He would call us. So the way I see it is, I am here another day, another moment, that means I still have work to do. There is one more life I need to connect with, one more act of service I need to do, one more day of obedience to my King. If I am still here, then that is one more day I can reach someone with the love of Jesus!

As we painted a small box to be a present ornament and tied a silver bow on top, I pondered what a beautiful gift Jesus gave us through His death. Jesus didn't want this pain. We don't want the pain of this world, but Jesus was willing to endure for the plan of His Father to be accomplished. Our task is nothing like the one Jesus had before Him. Surely we can handle another day without falling asleep, right? Surely we can stand up and keep a look out for Jesus, right? How betrayed Jesus must have already felt that the ones He was closest to on earth could not, or would not, carry out a simple task for Him. Jesus, I pray I will be a better servant to you. I don't want to sleep through my day while our enemy comes for You. I want to be close to You. I want You to know You can count on your servant Jennifer Moye. I am perfectly imperfect, but I am made in Your image. And through You I can do great, great things!

Day 21

A ROOSTER CROWS

This morning we found Elfie hanging out of one of the boys stockings. My creative skills are running out by day twenty-one. Today's lesson wasn't one that we laughed and played games about. Today's lesson talks of betrayal and denial. Is today's lesson about us?

While Jesus was still speaking, Judas arrived. He was one of the 12 disciples. A large crowd was with him. They were carrying swords and clubs. The chief priests and the elders of the people had sent them. Judas, who was going to hand Jesus over, had arranged a signal with them. "The one I kiss is the man," he said. "Arrest him." So Judas went to Jesus at once. He said, "Greetings, Rabbi!" And he kissed him.

Jesus replied, "Friend, do what you came to do."

Then the men stepped forward. They grabbed Jesus and arrested him. At that moment, one of Jesus' companions reached for his sword. He pulled it out and struck the slave of the high priest with it. He cut off the slave's ear.

"Put your sword back in its place," Jesus said to him. "All who use the sword will die by the sword. Do you think I can't ask my Father for help? He would send an army of more than 70,000 angels right away. But then how would the Scriptures come true? They say it must happen in this way."

At that time Jesus spoke to the crowd. "Am I leading a band of armed men against you?" he asked. "Do you have to come out with swords and clubs to capture me? Every day I sat in the temple courtyard teaching. And you didn't arrest me. But all this has happened so that the words of the prophets would come true." Then all the disciples left him and ran away.

Those who had arrested Jesus took him to Caiaphas, the high priest. The teachers of the law and the elders had come together there. Not too far away, Peter followed Jesus. He went right up to the courtyard of the high priest. He entered and sat down with the guards to see what would happen.

The chief priests and the whole Sanhedrin were looking for something to use against Jesus. They wanted to put him to death. But they did not find any proof, even though many false witnesses came forward.

Finally, two other witnesses came forward. They said, "This fellow claimed, 'I am able to destroy the temple of God. I can build it again in three days.'"

Then the high priest stood up. He asked Jesus, "Aren't you going to answer? What are these charges that these men are bringing against you?" But Jesus remained silent.

The high priest said to him, "I am commanding you in the name of the living God. May he judge you if you don't tell the truth. Tell us if you are the Messiah, the Son of God."

"You have said so," Jesus replied. "But here is what I say to all of you. From now on, you will see the Son of Man sitting at the right hand of the Mighty One. You will see the Son of Man coming on the clouds of heaven."

Then the high priest tore his clothes. He said, "He has spoken a very evil thing against God! Why do we need any more witnesses? You have heard him say this evil thing. What do you think?"

"He must die!" they answered.

Then they spit in his face. They hit him with their fists. Others slapped him. They said, "Prophesy to us, Messiah! Who hit you?"

Peter was sitting out in the courtyard. A female servant came to him. "You also were with Jesus of Galilee," she said.

But in front of all of them, Peter said he was not. "I don't know what you're talking about," he said.

Then he went out to the gate leading into the courtyard. There another servant saw him. She said to the people, "This fellow was with Jesus of Nazareth."

Again he said he was not. With a curse he said, "I don't know the man!"

After a little while, those standing there went up to Peter. "You must be one of them," they said. "The way you talk gives you away."

Then Peter began to curse and said to them, "I don't know the man!"

Right away a rooster crowed. Then Peter remembered what Jesus had said. "The rooster will crow," Jesus had told him. "Before it does, you will say three times that you don't know me." Peter went outside. He broke down and cried. (Matthew 26:47–75)

This is a lot to cover in one morning's attention span. We divided this passage into three parts. The first is Jesus's arrest. We learned yesterday that Jesus knew this was coming. It was not a surprise to Him. It was the disciples who were caught off guard, probably because they were sleepy-eyed from their naps. Today we see that one of Jesus's disciples, Judas, has turned on Him and is the one who points Jesus out to the guards to be arrested. "Would you ever do something like that to one of your friends, or even to Jesus?" I asked the boys. They were a bit in awe that one of the disciples would do this to Jesus. I explained to them that Judas was wrong in his actions, but that it came as no surprise to Jesus. He knew, and He knew it was all part of God's plan that had to be completed so that we could be forgiven.

Jesus also lets us know here that there is no need for violence. He calms the disciple who takes out his sword to defend Jesus. The boys agreed that they would do the same and defend Jesus from being arrested! Here, Jesus reminds us that He could call an army to defend Him at any time. But He didn't. He wasn't fighting or struggling against them. He had come to understand that this must happen.

The second part we talked about was Jesus's trail at the Sanhedrin. Here Jesus was accused of saying He was the Messiah when the people clearly thought He was not. Why didn't Jesus answer them or give them some type of miracle to prove who He was? Again I pointed out that Jesus did not deny His identity or try to save Himself. Jesus knew that He had to be crucified to complete His mission on earth. I asked the boys how it made them feel to hear how mean people were being to Jesus. They said words like sad, mad, and hurt. "Has anyone ever made fun of you for believing in Jesus?" I asked them. They answered no, but said if they did they would just "tell them they are wrong." This made me chuckle a little. We talked about different ways people might question us and our belief in God. Naturally this led perfectly into the last part of our story where Peter denies knowing Jesus three times before the rooster crowed.

"Would you ever deny believing in God like Peter did?" I asked. "Never!" It is hard for a four- and five-year-old mind to understand all of this but it isn't so hard for us grownups to imagine. Many of us have been in situations where it was not the "cool" thing to do to be a follower of Christ. I think we have all probably felt that same pressure Peter felt. How do we respond in those times? The boys asked why Peter would lie the way he did. I don't know exactly what Peter was thinking, but I explained to the boys that Peter was probably very afraid that if he was identified as a follower of Jesus he might be in trouble too. His answers came from fear. Peter was not willing to give up his own life to stand up for his relationship with Jesus. We talked a little about the world today and how in some places people get in a lot of trouble for believing in and worshiping God. Would Peter have been killed if he admitted to following Jesus? Maybe? I don't know, but I would hope that I would have been brave enough to proudly defend my Jesus.

As we painted a wooden rooster ornament an obnoxiously bright red, our conversation went on to topics like standing up for what we know is right and what we believe in. In a five-year-old's mind, I think this was hard to grasp. But for me it was a great reminder of times to come. I believe there will be a time, sooner than we probably know, where we will be asked the same questions Peter was asked. It is easy for me to sit here at my table and judge Peter for his answers and for hiding. It is easy until I am in that same situation with that same pressure. I have a family, maybe Peter did too. I feel pretty confident in saying that I wouldn't hesitate to recognize my love relationship with God. I hope that I nor my boys are ever in that situation, but I would be proud to mourn their sacrifice of standing up for Jesus!

If you are like Johnathan, you know what is coming tomorrow.

Day 22

ELFIE MEETS US AT THE CROSS

As Johnathan suspected, Elfie greeted us today with a colorful art project of a cross covered in pom-poms. While Elfie's cross was a bit more colorful than most, the boys loved that Elfie seemed to know where our story was going today as well.

The soldiers brought them to the place called the Skull. There they nailed Jesus to the cross. He hung between the two criminals. One was on his right and one was on his left. Jesus said, "Father, forgive them. They don't know what they are doing." The soldiers divided up his clothes by casting lots.

The people stood there watching. The rulers even made fun of Jesus. They said, "He saved others. Let him save himself if he is God's Messiah, the Chosen One."

The soldiers also came up and poked fun at him. They offered him wine vinegar. They said, "If you are the king of the Jews, save yourself."

A written sign had been placed above him. It read, this is the king of the Jews.

One of the criminals hanging there made fun of Jesus. He said, "Aren't you the Messiah? Save yourself! Save us!"

But the other criminal scolded him. "Don't you have any respect for God?" he said. "Remember, you are under the same sentence of death. We are being punished fairly. We are getting just what our actions call for. But this man hasn't done anything wrong."

Then he said, "Jesus, remember me when you come into your kingdom."

Jesus answered him, "What I'm about to tell you is true. Today you will be with me in paradise."

It was now about noon. Then darkness covered the whole land until three o'clock. The sun had stopped shining. The temple curtain was torn in two. Jesus called out in a loud voice, "Father, into your hands I commit my life." After he said this, he took his last breath.

A man named Joseph was a member of the Jewish Council. He was a good and honest man. Joseph had not agreed with what the leaders had decided and done. He was from Arimathea, a town in Judea. He himself was waiting for God's kingdom. Joseph went to Pilate and asked for Jesus' body. Joseph took it down and wrapped it in linen cloth. Then he placed it in a tomb cut in the rock. No one had ever been buried there. It was Preparation Day. The Sabbath day was about to begin.

The women who had come with Jesus from Galilee followed Joseph. They saw the tomb and how Jesus' body was placed in it. Then they went home. There they prepared spices and perfumes. But they rested on the Sabbath day in order to obey the Law. (Luke 23:33–46, 50–56)

This is a story the boys were pretty familiar with, and most of you probably are too. It's hard to talk about, isn't it? Every time I read this story, or watch a movie, or hear a sermon, it never stops being heartbreaking. And I pray it never will. Watching the boys go from a happy morning of finding Elfie to saddened faces of grief and pain was very hard. My purpose in this lesson was not to make them sad or make them feel guilty for all their sins. I believe it is absolutely necessary to understand what Jesus went through for us. Even at their young age, I want them to know that while Jesus had all the power to stop His suffering, He *chose* to remain in it for us . . . for them. It was brutal. It was unkind. It was not deserved. The criminals at Jesus's sides could even see that. I think the hardest part about today's lesson was not talking about tomorrow's lesson to cheer everyone up. But I think it is needed. I think we all need to remember what He went through for us all through the year, not just at Easter when we all watch the Passion movie. I think we should all wake up being humbled by what a high price was given for our redemption.

We each painted a wooden cross for our ornament and with each brush stroke we imagined what it must have been like to be on that hill that day. To watch darkness cover the land and to hear the thundering clap of God's mighty hand. What a heartbreaking scene that must have been. My favorite part of today was hearing Johnathan comment about the "storm" that came when Jesus took His last breath. With a very firm look, Johnathan sat up straight, crossed his arms, and said, "Well, I bet when God made the earth dark and that storm came and broke the temple thingy, I bet they all knew then! They all knew that they had done a bad thing and that Jesus was real!"

I hope today does not leave you sad, but instead leaves you feeling so enormously grateful and blessed by Jesus's act of sacrifice for you. You are not worthy, but He is and He loves each of us right where we are and just as we are. Thank Him today for the cross. Thank Him for saving you!

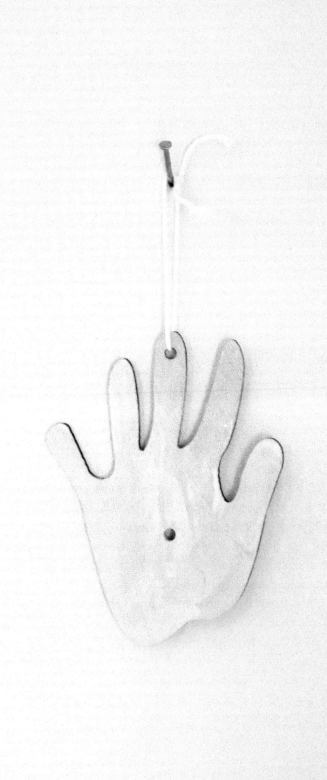

Day 23

A RESURRECTION CELEBRATION

This morning we woke to find Elfie sitting by the tomb. And to all of our amazement the tomb was empty! Elfie had found our Jenga blocks and had built a pretty awesome tomb out of them! No wonder Elfie has such a grin on his face! After yesterday's lesson on Jesus's death on the cross, the boys were jumping up and down in celebration!

Early on the first day of the week, Mary Magdalene went to the tomb. It was still dark. She saw that the stone had been moved away from the entrance. So she ran to Simon Peter and another disciple, the one Jesus loved. She said, "They have taken the Lord out of the tomb! We don't know where they have put him!"

So Peter and the other disciple started out for the tomb. Both of them were running. The other disciple ran faster than Peter. He reached the tomb first. He bent over and looked in at the strips of linen lying there. But he did not go in. Then Simon Peter came along behind him. He went straight into the tomb. He saw the strips of linen lying there. He also saw the funeral cloth that had been wrapped around Jesus' head. The cloth was still lying in its place. It was separate from the linen. The disciple who had reached the tomb first also went inside. He saw and believed. They still did not understand from Scripture that Jesus had to rise from the dead. Then the disciples went back to where they were staying.

But Mary stood outside the tomb crying. As she cried, she bent over to look into the tomb. She saw two angels dressed in white. They were seated where Jesus' body had been. One of them was where Jesus' head had been laid. The other sat where his feet had been placed.

They asked her, "Woman, why are you crying?"

"They have taken my Lord away," she said. "I don't know where they have put him." Then she turned around and saw Jesus standing there. But she didn't realize that it was Jesus.

He asked her, "Woman, why are you crying? Who are you looking for?"

She thought he was the gardener. So she said, "Sir, did you carry him away? Tell me where you put him. Then I will go and get him."

Jesus said to her, "Mary."

She turned toward him. Then she cried out in the Aramaic language, "Rabboni!" Rabboni means Teacher.

Jesus said, "Do not hold on to me. I have not yet ascended to the Father. Instead, go to those who believe in me. Tell them, 'I am ascending to my Father and your Father, to my God and your God.'"

Mary Magdalene went to the disciples with the news. She said, "I have seen the Lord!" And she told them that he had said these things to her.

On the evening of that first day of the week, the disciples were together. They had locked the doors because they were afraid of the Jewish leaders. Jesus came in and stood among them. He said, "May peace be with you!" Then he showed them his hands and his side. The disciples were very happy when they saw the Lord. (John 20:1–20)

While this is a story we usually hear about at Easter time, I think it is so crucial to understanding our salvation everyday as well. Jesus's resurrection is the cornerstone of our faith. Not only did He suffer and die on the cross for us, but in His unfathomable greatness He rose from that grave. Death could not hold him! The boys jumped up and down in amazement that Jesus had arisen.

Mary was the first one to find the tomb empty. I wonder how she felt finding the tomb that way. Obviously Scripture tells us she was afraid and thought that people had taken Jesus and placed Him somewhere else. I asked the boys what they would have thought if they were the first ones to arrive at the tomb that day. They answered that they would probably be afraid and not know where Jesus went.

When Mary looked up into the tomb the second time she did not see an empty tomb. Standing beside her she saw Jesus very much alive! How amazing that moment must have been to realize Jesus was indeed alive!

Our ornament today was a simple hand print with a nail hole in the middle to signify when Jesus showed the disciples His hands and has side to prove that it was He. As I watched Johnathan glide his paint brush over the hole in that hand print, I was overcome with emotion for what Christ has done for us. My little boy will live forever in heaven in the presence of Jesus not only because of that hole in that hand print but because of that empty tomb we just read about!

So many miracles and amazing things happen in the story of Jesus's life. The resurrection is, of course, one that a lot of people are familiar with. What surprised me the most about this lesson is that it seemed to be the first time my boys had heard it. Maybe it was just the first time it clicked within the story of Jesus's life? I know we have talked about the resurrection before at Easter, and of course when we talked with Johnathan about his salvation. But yet, they seemed so amazed and surprised that Jesus rose from the dead.

I am convicted that we need to celebrate Jesus's resurrection every day, not just on Easter. I want our boys to know the power of knowing they serve and love and are loved by a living God, not just a stature or martyr. Our God is alive! He is alive in us and around us! Thank you, Father God. Thank you.

Day 24

THE ROAD TO EMMAUS

Elfie had to follow us on our travels today as we drove to visit with family. The boys were worried he wouldn't know where to find us, but of course he did. He was hanging out near the stockings on Grandma's fireplace.

That same day two of Jesus' followers were going to a village called Emmaus. It was about seven miles from Jerusalem. They were talking with each other about everything that had happened. As they talked about those things, Jesus himself came up and walked along with them. But God kept them from recognizing him.

Jesus asked them, "What are you talking about as you walk along?"

They stood still, and their faces were sad. One of them was named Cleopas. He said to Jesus, "Are you the only person visiting Jerusalem who doesn't know? Don't you know about the things that have happened there in the last few days?"

"What things?" Jesus asked.

"About Jesus of Nazareth," they replied. "He was a prophet. He was powerful in what he said and did in the sight of God and all the people. The chief priests and our rulers handed Jesus over to be sentenced to death. They nailed him to a cross. But we had hoped that he was the one who was going to set Israel free. Also, it is the third day since all this happened. Some of our women amazed us too. Early this morning they went to the tomb. But they didn't find his body. So they came and told us what they had seen. They saw angels, who said Jesus was alive. Then some of our friends went to the tomb. They saw it was empty, just as the women had said. They didn't see Jesus' body there."

Jesus said to them, "How foolish you are! How long it takes you to believe all that the prophets said! Didn't the Messiah have to suffer these things and then receive his glory?" Jesus explained to them what was said about himself in all the Scriptures. He began with Moses and all the Prophets.

They approached the village where they were going. Jesus kept walking as if he were going farther. But they tried hard to keep him from leaving. They said, "Stay with us. It is nearly evening. The day is almost over." So he went in to stay with them.

He joined them at the table. Then he took bread and gave thanks. He broke it and began to give it to them. Their eyes were opened, and they recognized him. But then he disappeared from their sight. They said to each other, "He explained to us what the Scriptures meant. Weren't we excited as he talked with us on the road?" (Luke 24:13–32)

To understand this story correctly, we need to remember that this was Resurrection Day. Jesus has just risen from the grave that morning. This was the greatest event in the history of mankind and certainly the foundation of our Christian faith! This day should have been a celebration day, but these two men walking from Jerusalem to Emmaus seemed discouraged. Why would they be so discouraged when they had heard the reports that the tomb of Jesus was empty and He was alive? Johnathan knew right away. "They did not believe."

Disappointment must have filled their hearts with despair, since they had thought Jesus would be the one to save Israel. These disciples, like many other people today, saw the glory of the kingdom, but they fail to understand the suffering Jesus had to go through. These men didn't understand what God said in His Word about His plan and His promises. It is easy for us to sit here today and judge their disbelief, but what if that was us on that day? Would we believe? Their world had crumbled around them and they needed encouragement. I asked the boys if they would be sad like these men were. They agreed that they would be sad about Jesus dying as well.

Much like people today, these two disciples had all the evidence they needed to believe that He rose from the dead, but they walked in unbelief. Their real problem was not in their heads, but in their hearts. They needed a fresh understanding of the Word of God, and Jesus gave that understanding to them. The disciples from Emmaus were counting on Jesus to rescue Israel. Most Jews believed that the Old Testament prophecies pointed to a military and political Messiah. They believed that the Messiah would come to rule and reign at that time. They didn't realize that the Messiah had come to rescue people's souls. When Jesus died on the cross that week, they lost hope. They didn't understand that Jesus's death offered the greatest hope available.

Why did Jesus call these men foolish? Cleopas and his companion failed to believe and understand all that the prophets had written about the Messiah's suffering. That was the problem with most of the Jews of that day. They saw the Messiah as a conquering Redeemer, but they didn't see Him as a suffering servant. God promised us salvation through the suffering and death of His Son. God's offer of salvation will never disappoint us. Jesus will never let us down. Because He now lives, we are encouraged, never disappointed, to know that everyone who believes in Him will be saved (Romans 10:10–11).

After the two disciples expressed their discouragement in what had happened, Jesus answered them by going to Scripture and applying it to His ministry. They needed the encouragement of God's word. When we are discouraged or puzzled by questions or problems, we can find encouragement in the promises of God's word. Romans 15:4 tells us, "For whatever was written in earlier times were written for our instruction, that through perseverance and the encouragement of the Scriptures we might have hope."

As Jesus began to walk away, the disciples asked Him to come home with them. I think they had been encouraged by the word of God and desired for the blessing to last. The more we receive the word of God, the more we want the fellowship of the word of God. Jesus opened the Scriptures to them and then He opened their eyes so that they recognized Him. Now they knew for themselves that He was alive.

Vanishing from their sight, Jesus left them with the comfort of knowing that He was alive and that God's word was true. Jesus had made things very plain and clear to them; a divine heat and a divine light burned in their souls. Their hearts burned within, kindled with a holy fire of faith toward their Savior, Jesus. God's word can warm our hearts with the peace of His promises too. It both instructs and comforts us, giving us a holy desire and devotion within our heart to worship Him. The disciples were so excited and overwhelmed with joy that they made their way back to Jerusalem that very hour. They had seen Jesus, and God's promises were true. There was no time to waste; they couldn't wait to tell their friends what had happened.

We painted a red heart as our ornament today, and I asked the boys, "Has Jesus made a difference in your life?" I ask you the same question. These two men were changed and they wanted others to experience the same hope and joy which is found through Jesus and

His word. There are so many people around us who live a life without hope, filled with discouragement. Jesus can make the life-changing difference, but we need to tell them. Jesus is alive, and we can trust in His promises.

Day 25

THE BEST CHRISTMAS GIFT

O n this Christmas morning, Elfie was in the same spot he was yesterday. Umm, yeah, he must have forgotten to move. He did, however, remember to bring us a new craft and Bible lesson. And with all of the excitement that Christmas morning brings, it was so great to make the time to dig into our last Bible story for this year!

Theophilus, I wrote about Jesus in my earlier book. I wrote about all he did and taught until the day he was taken up to heaven. Before Jesus left, he gave orders to the apostles he had chosen. He did this through the Holy Spirit. After his suffering and death, he appeared to them. In many ways he proved that he was alive. He appeared to them over a period of 40 days. During that time he spoke about God's kingdom. One day Jesus was eating with them. He gave them a command. "Do not leave Jerusalem," he said. "Wait for the gift my Father promised. You have heard me talk about it. John baptized with water. But in a few days you will be baptized with the Holy Spirit."

Then the apostles gathered around Jesus and asked him a question. "Lord," they said, "are you going to give the kingdom back to Israel now?"

He said to them, "You should not be concerned about times or dates. The Father has set them by his own authority. But you will receive power when the Holy Spirit comes on you. Then you will tell people about me in Jerusalem, and in all Judea and Samaria. And you will even tell other people about me from one end of the earth to the other."

After Jesus said this, he was taken up to heaven. The apostles watched until a cloud hid him from their sight.

While he was going up, they kept on looking at the sky. Suddenly two men dressed in white clothing stood beside them. "Men of Galilee," they said, "why do you stand here looking at the sky? Jesus has been taken away from you into heaven. But he will come back in the same way you saw him go." (Acts 1)

Over the last month, we have followed the life of Jesus. Over the last couple days, we have seen Him betrayed, beaten, put to death, and we saw him rise from the grave. Today we learn that Jesus was with the people for forty days after He rose from the dead. In this passage we learn about the gift that God gives to us in the form of the Holy Spirit. We learn that the Holy Spirit will be with us until Christ comes again in the same way He left. This was an interesting lesson to talk with the boys about.

The boys loved to talk about and picture Jesus floating up to the heavens much like a balloon floats up into the clouds. Our ornament was to make a white cloud from scrap felt and some cotton balls. We imagined how awesome and maybe confusing it would have been to watch this all happen that day. Our favorite song this year has been "There is Power in the Name of Jesus," so we really enjoyed verse 8! The Holy Spirit is alive in us and gives us *power*!

We have talked a lot about the Holy Spirit and how that is how Jesus lives in our hearts and is here with us even though we cannot see Him. The boys understand that as much as a four- and five-year-old can. We have not really talked about His return before though. Matthew 2:19–20 tells us:

> *So you must go and make disciples of all nations. Baptize them in the name of the Father and of the Son and of the Holy Spirit. Teach them to obey everything I have commanded you. And you can be sure that I am always with you, to the very end."*

I asked the boys what they thought Jesus would want us to do while we wait for Him to return. "Tell people about Jesus." Correct answer. Win for this whole devotional idea! Yes! It was so important to Jesus that we tell others about Him that it was the last thing He told the disciples and all the people around Him. It is important! It is our job to take all that we have learned about Him and tell everyone we know. Jesus will be with us, by the Holy Spirit, and we have all the power we need to do whatever we need to do to make Him famous. There is power in the name of Jesus!

End

About the Author

Jennifer Moye writes from a place of transparency and with the heart of a mom passionate about God's will for her family. Her candid sense of humor makes her writing easy and enjoyable to read. She speaks with an authentic style that will have you laughing with relatability yet challenged to step up to your next highest calling in your walk with God. Jennifer is wife to an airman and mom to three rambunctious little boys. With excitement on a daily basis and grace around every corner, she believes we are meant to live this life in community with others and with the mercy to mess up and try again and again. Being a mom is hard, but it is also one of the greatest callings we can have in this life. Her ministry to women is relevant and heartfelt with her core passion being that we learn to glorify our God in our parenting, our marriage, and in our everyday lives.

Join Jennifer's community online at:

www.jennifermoye.com
www.facebook.com/jennifermoye
www.twitter.com/jenmoyewrites
www.pinterest.com/jenmoyewrites

CPSIA information can be obtained
at www.ICGtesting.com
Printed in the USA
LVOW06s1727121117
555851LV00015B/161/P